Women, Technology
and Innovation

Other Titles of Interest

BAEHR, H.
Women and Media

EICHLER, M. & SCOTT, H.
Women in Futures Research

KRAMARAE, C.
The Voices and Words of Women and Men

NELSON, N.
Why Has Development Neglected Rural Women?

SPENDER, D.
Men's Studies Modified

Women, Technology and Innovation

Edited by
Joan Rothschild

PERGAMON PRESS

OXFORD · NEW YORK · TORONTO · SYDNEY · PARIS · FRANKFURT

U.K.	Pergamon Press Ltd., Headington Hill Hall, Oxford OX3 0BW, England
U.S.A.	Pergamon Press Inc., Maxwell House, Fairview Park, Elmsford, New York 10523, U.S.A.
CANADA	Pergamon Press Canada Ltd., Suite 104, 150 Consumers Rd., Willowdale, Ontario M2J 1P9, Canada
AUSTRALIA	Pergamon Press (Aust.) Pty. Ltd., P.O. Box 544, Potts Point, N.S.W. 2011, Australia
FRANCE	Pergamon Press SARL, 24 rue des Ecoles, 75240 Paris, Cedex 05, France
FEDERAL REPUBLIC OF GERMANY	Pergamon Press GmbH, 6242 Kronberg-Taunus, Hammerweg 6, Federal Republic of Germany

First edition 1982

Published as a special issue of the journal *Women's Studies International Quarterly* Volume 4, Number 3 and supplied to subscribers as part of their normal subscription.

ISBN 0 08 028943 6

Printed in Great Britain by A. Wheaton & Co. Ltd., Exeter

CONTENTS

EDITORIAL

The work in this issue represents a new field in women's studies, that of women and technology. Although focusing specifically on technology, the issue includes work on women and science as well. While the distinction can be made between science as discovery for its own sake and technology as being 'applied' or 'practical', the two are inextricably linked at both practical and philosophical levels. Scientific and technological innovations interact dialectically for actual discovery and invention, and science and technology share deep philosophical roots. That science and technology have traditionally been viewed as masculine realms adds a critical dimension for feminist analysis and forms an underlying premise for the contributions to this issue.

Much of the work included became known to me through my own research into theoretical and philosophical women/technology issues and on technology and domestic labor, and through panels I have organized for a number of feminist studies conferences. The articles, Women's Studies Section, and book reviews present some of the major categories in the field. Margaret Alic on women scientists in ancient Egypt, Autumn Stanley on early women inventors in horticulture, and Helen Irvin on Shaker women's inventions are examples of compensatory history, which attempts to restore to women their neglected and rightful places in the history of each field. [Stanley's forthcoming book, *Mothers of Invention* (Scarecrow Press, Metuchen, New Jersey, 1982), from which her article is adapted, promises to correct the record in many more areas]. Philosophical and feminist theory issues are examined by Sally Hacker on mind–body dualisms, in my review essay on woman and nature, and in the Women's Studies Section, in particular the article by Ynestra King. Contemporary issues, including women in the labor force and high technology, are explored by Jan Zimmerman on high technology, women and the future; Erik Arnold, Linda Birke and Wendy Faulkener on micro-processing; and by Hacker on the culture of engineering, plus book reviews on reproductive technology and on feminist utopias. Missing from this list and from the issue is technology and women in the Third World, where technological innovation, in disrupting traditional economic and cultural patterns, has often adversely affected the condition of women. New scholarship here for the English-speaking world has been less readily available or else the technology issues are subsumed under larger development and political concerns.

Whether analyzing the effects of technology *on* women or the role of women *in* technological development, research in this field reveals the critical need to reassess the values and assumptions underlying a Western-based modern science and technology. Both implicitly and explicitly, the work on women, technology and innovation represented in the following pages challenges and questions these values.

JOAN ROTHSCHILD

Women's Studies Int. Quart., Vol. 4, No. 3, pp. 289–304, 1981.
Printed in Great Britain.

0148–0685/81/030289–16$02.00/0
Pergamon Press Ltd.

DAUGHTERS OF ISIS, DAUGHTERS OF DEMETER: WHEN WOMEN SOWED AND REAPED

Autumn Stanley

Wilbur Hot Springs, Wilbur Springs, CA 95987, U.S.A.

Synopsis—Evidence from anthropology, archaeology, mythology and primate ethology indicates that women were the main gatherers, processors, and storers of plant food from earliest human times onward, and thus the most logical ones to have invented the tools and methods involved in this work, from digging stick and carrier to cooking and sophisticated methods of detoxification. Anthropologists now generally agree that women also invented horticulture, the intentional cultivation of food plants in specified areas. This paper details women's early accomplishments in food-gathering, processing, and cultivative technology, including the domestication and improvement of all the world's major food plants, early irrigation, and early ploughs, documents the trend toward male dominance of cultivation as a society depends progressively more upon cultivation for its diet; and presents a composite theory to explain the trend. A population explosion and a patriarchal religious takeover are important factors.

'. . . Women with their children or grandchildren toddling behind explored the thick growth of plants encircling their homes. They learned eventually which bore fruits that sated hunger, which bore leaves and roots that chased illness and pain, and which worked magic on the eye, mouth, and head.

The Goddess Demeter watched fondly as the mortals learned more and more about Her plants. Seeing that their lives were difficult and their food supply sporadic. She was moved to give them the gift of wheat. She showed them how to plant the seed, cultivate, and finally harvest the wheat and grind it. Always the mortals entrusted the essential process of planting food to the women, in the hope that their fecundity of womb might be transferred to the fields they touched.'

This retelling of the pre-Hellenic myth of Demeter (Spretnak, 1978; pp. 103–104) compresses several thousands of years of human history into two brief paragraphs.[1] It also tells us something that anthropology has just recently concluded: that women were the original plant experts, the major providers of food for gathering–hunting tribes, and thus the logical ones to have invented the intentional cultivation of plants for food, i.e. horticulture and eventually agriculture.

In this article I look at this same span of several thousand years in somewhat more detail, and from the single focus of food technology: the gathering, processing (including cooking), cultivation, and storage of food. I divide the time into three periods—pre-horticultural, horticultural, and agricultural. Women dominated the technology of the first two periods, and have contributed far more than is generally recognized to the third.[2]

---

[1] Demeter is the Greek analogue of Isis, who gave the Egyptians grain (as well as linen, their world-famed enbalming process, and sail for ships). The mysteries of the two goddesses were the same (Spretnak, 1978; p. 99).

[2] A more extensive discussion of women's role in the technology of cultivation appears in my forthcoming book *Mothers of Invention* (Stanley, 1982).

However, men have come to dominate the technology, or at least the high technology, of agriculture in much of the world. In view of women's early pre-eminence in the cultivative role and its technology, this is puzzling. In view of the crucial importance of agriculture and the settled lifestyle in human history, the development is also extremely important. How and why did this shift in technological dominance come about? In discussing the change from horticulture to agriculture, I will supply a missing or neglected piece in the puzzle, and use it to build a takeover theory that seems to answer questions left unanswered by earlier theories.

My sources and underlying assumptions are drawn from mythology,[3] early historians, primate ethology, archaeology, and anthropology, specifically work on division of labor by sex in surviving agricultural and pre-agricultural tribes. I have relied most heavily on division-of-labor evidence in making my basic assumption about the pre-horticultural and horticultural periods, which is that, all else being equal, *the workers invented their tools*. And women were the plant workers. From earliest times until at least the horticultural period, as mythology and anthropology agree, women were largely responsible for the gathering, processing (Tanner and Zihlmann, 1976; Zihlmann, 1978; Murdock and Provost, 1973; pp. 207, 210), storing, and eventually for the cultivation (Martin and Voorhies, 1975; p. 214) of plant foods.[4] Anthropologists now generally agree that women invented horticulture (Rohrlich-Leavitt, 1977; p. 38; Martin and Voorhies, p. 216). I further and more specifically assume that any food-gathering, processing, or storage tool or process, as well as any cultivative tool or method, found in a people's tool kit or repertoire by the early horticultural period was most likely invented by a woman.

PRE-HORTICULTURAL INVENTIONS

It is no accident that food comes first in the traditional list of human priorities: food, clothing, shelter. Indeed, so obvious a need can be taken for granted, and the technology connected with it dismissed as a non-technology.[5] Yet the females who learned how to gather, transport, and make edible the staple foods of early human clans and tribes were on the cutting edge of technology at that time. Moreover, without their inventions, the human animal would have little more chance for survival and high civilization than its primate relatives.

What evidence do we have that these early inventors were female? Both proto-human sexes would have gathered plant foods in order to survive from day to day. However, females' gathering would be different from males'—more highly motivated, and more of a 'social role' from the start in that females were usually gathering for one or more offspring as well as for

---

[3] Mythology can be relevant in at least two ways: insofar as it reflects what actually happened in ancient times (including reflections of and attempts to explain social change), and insofar as deities are credited with specific technological innovations. Real women who invented such vital things as medicines, pottery, weaving—or horticulture—might be deified (as with the Empress Se-ling-she and silk in China); or these accomplishments might be added to the attributes of an existing deity such as Isis or Athena. The important point here is that the sex of the deity credited presumably reveals the sex of the anonymous inventor.

[4] Of course it can be argued that women were the workers of the period, and thus very likely invented not only tools having to do with plants and plant food, but all the early peaceful arts and the tools and methods pertaining to them (Mason, 1894; Mozans, 1913); for it was probably not only among the Australian aborigines that 'Man's work is to hunt and fish and then sit down. Woman's work is all else' (Reed, 1975; p. 106).

[5] Compare Murdock and Provost's statement (p. 210) that 'One can, of course, name activities that are strictly feminine (i.e. limited to women in division of labor), e.g. nursing and infant care, but they fall outside the range of technological pursuits'. Unfortunately for women's technological history to date, this attitude is more prevalent than the one shown by Otis T. Mason in writing an entire book on cradles.

themselves.[6] Females, as the more pressed by necessity, would thus be more likely to innovate and improve. Moreover, since the earliest social units probably consisted of mothers and their offspring, with peripheral adult males, females would be more likely than males to transmit their inventions to the next generation (Tanner and Zihlmann, 1976; pp. 599, 604). We also have some interesting evidence from primate ethology, the study of behavior among our nearest animal relatives. Jane Goodall found that among the chimpanzees, with whom we share more than 99 per cent of our genes, females use tools more often and for longer time periods than males (Tanner and Zihlmann, 1976; pp. 591, 593).

Division-of-labor evidence is also strong. Among the 185 societies included in a standard cross-cultural sample of societies, the gathering of wild vegetable foods was predominantly female in 42 societies and exclusively female in 65 others, giving a worldwide index (a weighted composite average percentage) of female participation of 80.3. Preparation (processing) of vegetable foods and cooking had even higher scores: preparation was predominantly female in 21 societies and exclusively so in 145 others; cooking was predominantly female in 63 societies and exclusively so in 117 others, giving female-participation indices of 94.3 and 91.7 respectively (Murdock and Provost, 1973; pp. 207, 210).

The Pre-horticultural period is that first 99 per cent of the 2,000,000-odd years of human history during which we foraged (gathered, hunted, fished) for our food rather than cultivating or buying it (F. Lee and De Vore, 1968; p. 3). Anthropological data have upset two traditional assumptions about this period: that hunting was more important than gathering, and that foraging life was nasty, brutish and short, a constant struggle for food. Worldwide (except for the sub-Arctic), hunting provides only 20–40 per cent of the forager's diet (R. Lee and De Vore, 1968; p. 7), which means that the women's gathering provides 60–80 per cent of the diet! After close observation of the !Kung foragers at least one anthropologist concluded that foraging society was, in fact, 'the original affluent society' (R. Lee and DeVore, 1968; p. 85), and also a leisured society. !Kung women could gather all the food they needed in 2 or 3 days a week (R. Lee and DeVore, 1968; p. 33), and wild wheat grew so abundantly in the Near East that a person could probably gather a year's supply in about 3 weeks (Doster III *et al.*, 1978; p. 54).

Among the many inventions most certainly attributable to women during the Pre-horticultural period are (1) food-gathering inventions such as the digging stick, the carrying sling or bag, the reaping knife or sickle, and other knives; (2) food-processing inventions such as the mortar and pestle or pounder, winnowing methods, grain-roasting tray, querns (grinders for grain), washing to remove grit, detoxification (or removal of bitterness), and some forms of cooking (including ovens in some areas); and (3) food-storage inventions such as baskets, clay-lined storage pits, drying and smoking of food, and preservation with honey.

Let us look at one example of each category: the digging stick, cooking, and clay-lined storage pits. To understand the technological advance represented by the digging stick, consider digging up a yam with your bare hands. In order to get a yam $\frac{1}{2}$ in. thick and 1 ft long out of the ground, you might have to dig a hole more than 1 ft long and 2 ft deep (Reed, 1975; p. 107). Yams can grow several feet long. The digging stick opens up an entirely new source of food—the underground— containing not only roots and tubers that may become a staple

---

[6] Nancy Tanner and Adrienne Zihlmann (1976), in fact, hypothesize that it is this gathering for and sharing with others that gave rise to what we now call society, rather than male cooperation in hunting, which was sporadic rather than daily (pp. 599 ff). Notice, however, that both theories trace the beginnings of society to a food-related activity.

starch, but insect grubs that can provide scarce protein. The fire-hardening of the digging stick's point is also an invention—and the first spear may even have been a digging stick hurled in anger or fear. Women may or may not have invented the means of making a fire at will,[7] but no one seriously disputes the overwhelming division-of-labor evidence that women invented cooking. Women's clever inventions (Kroeber, 1964; p. 25) of steatite (soapstone) griddles and pots (Mason, 1894; pp. 33, 144), of waterproof cooking baskets and the use of hot stones to boil mush or liquids, of parching—indeed of all the early forms of cooking and the implements needed for them—were the high technology of their day. Soapstone, for example, will not crack in the fire. Cooking makes inedible foods edible, partly indigestible foods more digestible, and tough foods manageable for toothless oldsters. Thus cooking not only helps a tribe survive from day to day on less food intake, but improves its chances for cultural transmission.

Clay-lined storage pits, used by the Yahi Indians of California (Kroeber, 1964; p. 107) and as early as 10,000 BC in the Middle East (Mellaart, 1965; p. 30), can be made nearly waterproof. In some areas they may have imparted an antibiotic to grain stored in them, reducing the users' rate of disease.[8]

HORTICULTURAL INVENTIONS

The horticultural period begins in any society when people start intentionally planting the seeds or cuttings of favored food plants in specific areas around a camp rather than travelling for miles to gather from them wherever they naturally grow. In short, as the Latin name indicates (*hortus* = garden), it begins with the first gardens. Horticulture exists in two stages: simple or shifting cultivation (gardens are cleared, cultivated for a year or two, then allowed to revert to brush or forest for long fallow periods); and true horticulture (semi-intensive agricultural limited mainly to vegetables and/or fruit trees rather than field crops) (Murdock and White, 1969; p. 363). Its earliest beginnings may date back 100,000 years, especially as the first of these two stages is compatible with nomadic or semi-nomadic lifestyles.

The major woman's invention of this period—and indeed perhaps of all time (Hawkes, 1976; p. 46)—is the invention of horticulture itself. Without precise documentation about a process that occurred many times in various parts of the world, in some cases taking thousands of years, we can only speculate as to how the shift to cultivation was made. The genesis no doubt was accidental. Women returning to camp from gathering might spill seeds or roots or cuttings, or discard half-eaten fruits on ground disturbed days or weeks before by their digging sticks. Subsequently, they might spill water from water-hauling along the route, and/or rain would soon fall; they or their children might stop to relieve themselves on the

---

[7] Mason (1894) and H. J. Mozans (1913), among others, are certain that they did, or at least that they were the first to control it (Boulding, 1976; pp. 78–80). The Prometheus myth is late, and only one of many on the origin of fire. The numerous female fire and hearth deities and the myths in which men stole fire not from the gods but from women (Sir James George Frazer, 1930, e.g. pp. 25, 40 ff), or in which women stole or were given fire (Kroeber, 1964; p. 79; Sokolov, 1978; p. 34), give another view. Most interesting of all, the name Prometheus comes from the Sanskrit word for the fire-making instrument called a fire-drill. Thus the myth may merely be saying that by inventing the fire-drill mortals took fire from the control of the gods (or fate or chance) and brought it under human control.

[8] A University of Massachusetts team of anthropologists discovered tetracycline in bone samples taken from a Sudanese burial ground where the Nubian population of about 350–550 AD had an extremely low rate of infectious disease. The researchers proposed that the antibiotic derived naturally from mold-like bacteria called streptomycetes in the mud grain bins where they stored grain. Although these Nilotic people were at least at the horticultural stage of development, the Yahi were foragers (*An Ancient People's Antibiotic*, 1980).

journey. After a short interval, or upon the group's next visit to the campsite, they might begin to notice small stands of their favored food plants springing up along their usual gathering routes. This might have happened in or near a food-preparation area, a burial ground, a garbage heap or midden, or in any other area of the camp where the combination of seeds or other propagative material and disturbed or fertilized or watered ground was present.

The crucial step was making the causal connection and deciding to do intentionally what had happened accidentally. And the person best prepared by expertise, daily work opportunity, and necessity to take that step in each group was almost always a woman.

In the process of developing horticulture women:

(a) domesticated plants; in so doing, they invented selective breeding, vastly improved the yield and other characteristics of cultivated plants, discovered propagation by shoots and cuttings, and invented such modern-sounding horticultural techniques as seedling beds;

(b) began to use fire as a systematic land-clearing tool;

(c) invented cultivating tools: hoe, spade or shovel, early plough;

(d) improved their food-gathering or harvesting tools: the carrying bag becomes a basket, etc.;

(e) improved their food-processing tools and methods: sophisticated grinders, rotary querns, threshing tools and methods, ceramic husking tray (Mesopotamia, 8000–5000 BC), other grain hullers; more complex detoxification apparatus and methods; pre-digestion of soybean cake, etc.;

(f) improved their food-storage inventions: baskets, clay granaries, storage houses on stilts;

(g) invented techniques for processing plant fibers if they had not already done so;

(h) invented early forms of irrigation;

(i) invented fertilizer;

(j) domesticated some animals; and

(k) next most significant to inventing horticulture itself, invented and practised environmentally sound techniques of cultivation: agriculture without tillage, crop rotation, fallow periods, land reclamation by tree planting or return to natural vegetation, mulching, terracing, and contour planting.

To illustrate from part of this impressive catalog:

Domestication and improvement of plants. Breaking the ground and sowing a crop is first proved at Mureybet, Mesopotamia, before 8000 BC (Hawkes, 1976; p. 49; Mellaart, 1973; pp. 45–47). By 8000 BC the inhabitants of Jericho in Palestine had grainfields and vegetable plots (Hawkes, 1976; p. 40). One of the first changes women made in cereal grains was to select for those that did not shed their seed in the wind or at a touch (Hawkes, 1976; p. 39). By 6000 BC the people of Çatal Hüyük in present-day Turkey had already developed bread wheat (*Triticum aestivum*) from Emmer wheat, and a naked six-row barley from the simpler two-row hulled barley (Mellaart, 1965; p. 202). Both of these were hybrids. Women harvesters must have noticed these especially fine specimens and saved them for seed stock.[9]

Of the hundreds of thousands of known plant species, 30 provide almost 85 per cent of all human food by weight, plus 95 per cent of our calories and protein (Vietmayer, 1979; p. 26). Some 75 per cent of all human food energy, in fact, comes from just eight cereals—wheat, rice, maize, barley, oats, sorghum, millet, and rye—and the first three account for 75 per cent of

---

[9] Or as offerings to the Goddess. This is one way that selective breeding might have arisen, as women saved especially fat ears of grain to devote to their deity. Such a custom could also have led naturally to the later practice of storing agricultural surpluses in the temples.

that 75 per cent. All eight were not only domesticated by women in this horticultural stage, but so much changed from their wild ancestors that botanists have sometimes been hard put to discover those ancestors.

Women have also improved the root crops on which much of the world subsists. Wild yams as gathered by the Australian aborigines were about the size of a cigar, whereas the cultivated yams grown by Melanesian women may be 6 ft long and 1 ft or more thick (Chapple and Coon, 1942; pp. 174–175). Indeed, the first cradle of agriculture possibly was not the Near East with its grasses but southern Asia with its yam and taro. These two root crops may have been cultivated there as early as 13,000–9000 BC (Doster *et al.*, 1978; p. 54).

Less well known are some of the more nutritious plants domesticated by horticultural woman and only now being rediscovered by modern scientists searching for more nutritious staple crops that will grow with less input of fertilizer and energy: the high-protein grain quinoa; the Andean lupine, tarwi; and the winged bean of New Guinea, for example. The winged bean is a veritable wonder plant with edible pods, tendrils, leaves, flowers, roots, and seeds providing a whole menu of spinach-, green-bean-, potato-, and soybean-like foods that contain vitamins A and E and as much protein and edible oil in the seeds as soybeans. Further, as a legume, this plant can manufacture its own nitrogen (essential for plant growth and a main ingredient in most fertilizers) from the air (Vietmayer, 1979; pp. 26–27).

Cultivating tools. From the hoes that they had invented by attaching a shell, a deer's shoulder-blade, or another stick to their digging sticks, women developed the earliest ploughs. The association of women with the plough may be a surprising one because of the physical strength needed for modern ploughing. But horticultural woman, trained from childhood as burden-bearer for the tribe, was very little weaker than a man and sometimes even stronger, as both anthropology and mythology attest (Mason, 1894; Ch. 6, p. 8; Reed, 1975; pp. 122–124; Davis, 1971; pp. 93–95). These early scratch ploughs were much more like early hoes than is generally recognized (see Fig. 1), and were not intended to turn the soil over but, as their name suggests, merely to make a shallow furrow. Moreover, in at least two places where these ploughs arose (The Middle East and Mediterranean Europe) the soil was of the light loess variety, consisting of finely pulverized rock dust from old glaciers (Hawkes, 1976; p. 16; Doster *et al.*, 1978; p. 69).

According to Otis T. Mason, an early twentieth century Curator of Ethnology at the Smithsonian Museum, and one of the few authorities on anthropology to look at the history of technology from the viewpoint of women's accomplishments, long before the European explorers came, 'women in America, Africa, and the Indo-Pacific were farmers, and had learned to use the digging stick, the hoe, and even a rude plough' (Mason, 1894; pp. 24–25). Mason specifically cites the nineteenth century explorer David Livingstone, who saw in Africa a double-handled hoe that women dragged through the ground.

Western mythology too supports women's invention of the plough, as both Athena and Minerva are specifically credited with inventing the plough, and Ceres, whose name gives us the word 'cereal', with both plough and ploughshare.

Food-processing inventions. Four impressive ones are (1) detoxification and debittering technology, (2) a sophisticated corn (maize)-processing method, (3) the rotary quern, and (4) a soybean-processing technology.

(1) Many of the world's staple foods are poisonous or indigestible or too bitter to eat—or all three—in their natural state. Olives, acorns, yams, manioc or cassava, taro, and sago are major examples. Olives demand a very complicated leaching process in several different baths of water, during which they must be kept from molding or rotting—or a treatment with

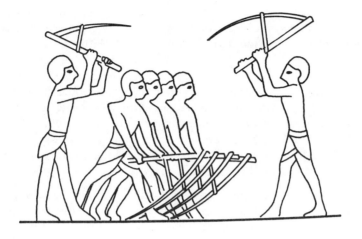

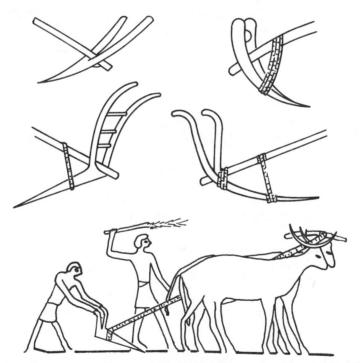

FIG. 1. Ancient Egyptian hoes (above) and ploughs (below), reproduced from Michael Partridge, *Farm Tools Through the Ages*, p. 36.

lye and then a somewhat shorter leaching process. Acorns must also be leached extensively, and North American Indian women invented ingenious ways to do this, including leaving acorns in net bags in streams over a season, or washing the pounded acorn flour in a sand filter near a stream or in a special basket made for the purpose. A specific example is the following method and apparatus for detoxifying manioc. The bitter manioc (cassava) tubers that are the staple starch for 200 million people in South America and Africa contain prussic (hydrocyanic) acid. The tubers must be either peeled, grated, and washed through several waters, or leached several days in a stream to soften them and loosen the peeling. Then the poisonous juices must be squeezed and strained out of the pulp, which is then sieved, or for the remaining large pieces, rubbed in mortar and pestle. The resulting damp meal still contains enough prussic acid to cause severe gastritis and must be toasted on a griddle or baked into cakes (heat drives off the rest of the volatile acid). Guyana Indian women have invented a device to aid them in this laborious process:

> 'One woman, squatting on her hams and armed with a big knife, peels off the skin of the root and washes it. Another woman, grasping one of the roots with both hands, scrapes it up and down an oblong board or grater studded with small fragments of stone like a nutmeg grater. . . . The rhythmic "swish" caused by the scraping is the chief sound in the house, for the labour is too heavy to permit talking. The grated cassava is placed into a long sieve or *matapie* so woven that a weight on the bottom will compress and open the sides, and we have press and strainer in one. The cassava, saturated with its poisonous juices, is forced into this matapie and suspended from one of the beams of the house. Through a loop in the bottom of the matapie a heavy pole is passed, one end of which rests on the ground. A woman now sits on the pole, and her weight stretches the strainer and forces the poisonous juice, which is caught in a vessel below. . . . The cassava is taken from the matapie, broken, sifted, and baked into griddle cakes, which are dried in the sun' [Mason, 1895 (1902); pp. 38–40].

Mundurucú women of Brazil in the twentieth century still use a very similar process and apparatus (Murphy and Murphy, 1974; pp. 8–12, 123–127), as do the Tupinambá (Sokolov, 1978; pp. 34, 38).

Notice the several inventions involved: the grater, the combined sieve and press, the griddle, and, among the Mundurucú, a spatula to turn the toasting flour and keep it from burning (Murphy and Murphy, p. 12). The matapie is a truly remarkable invention in that it not only combines the functions of press and sieve, but can be compared to the screw, and uses a lever principle as well [Mason, 1895 (1902); p. 60].

(2) A multiple metate for corn-processing was devised by the Moki (Hopi) Indian women of southwestern North America. These women, who had 50 ways of preparing corn (maize) for food, ground the kernels to the proper fineness for each kind of food by means of a four-part grinding box made of sandstone slabs mortared with clay. The 7-ft-long box has a metate with a different grinding surface and a muller of corresponding grain for each of the four compartments, the roughest for the coarse meal at one end, and the smoothest for the fine meal at the other. The box is set up near a wall so that the women can brace their feet while grinding, and the metates are set in the compartments at an angle of about 45°, plastered in firmly with clay (Mason, 1894; pp. 143–144).

(3) The rotary quern, a revolving hand mill for grinding grain, consists of two heavy circular stones turning one atop the other, with a hole in the top stone for pouring in the grain, and a handle or crank affixed for turning it. The rotary quern is significant not only as a

technological achievement *per se*, but as one of the possible antecedents of the wheel[10] and as the forerunner in design of the large animal-, wind-, and water-powered mills. The crank, which may appear first on querns, is also an important invention in the history of mechanical technology. One historian of technology ranks it second only to the wheel (White, 1978; pp. 17, 18).[11] Women invented such mills in various parts of the world, notably Ireland and Palestine (Mason, 1894; pp. 21, 23).

(4) In a world short of protein, Indonesian women have devised a processing method that makes available 20 per cent more of the protein in soybeans. After hulling and soaking the beans, they inoculate the mass with fungus spores and incubate them for a time before cutting into cakes. The fungus 'pre-digests' some of the molecules, breaking proteins into amino acids and fat into fatty acids, making them more available to the human digestive system (BBC 1 TV, 1979).

In all of the thousands of years that women were exclusive or predominant cultivators of the earth, most of the techniques they invented were environmentally sound. The Mundurucú, for example, practise a slash-and-burn form of cultivation, but use a garden only 2 years before letting it revert to jungle for renewal. Moreover, they know their soil well, classifying it into types from black through red to clay, with sub-types according to the amount of sand present. Only in the black soil can the women grow melons, beans, and rice. Both red soil and black is good for maize, but the clay soils support mainly manioc. Within 20 years of abandonment, the erstwhile garden is a luxuriant secondary forest; within 50 years no one but a forestry expert, or an Indian, could tell the garden had ever been there. Since they supplement their gardening with gathering, fishing, and hunting, and their population is fairly stable, the Mundurucú can afford to wait the necessary 2 decades before clearing any given patch again (Murphy and Murphy, pp. 60–62).

Yokaia women of Central California, in the process of cultivating their small personal gardens of corn (maize), invented an extreme form of agriculture without tillage—now being advocated to cope with the massively exploitive cultivative patterns created by males in recent centuries. These Indian women used neither plough nor hoe, but sat down beside each hill of corn and dug the earth deeply and rubbed it fine with their hands. Their yields were greater than those of the white settlers planting in the same region. Moreover, by disturbing such a tiny area, they could control not only erosion but weed growth as well (Mason, 1894; p. 147; Triplett Jr. and Van Doren Jr., 1977).

These methods, of which hundreds of other examples could be given, respect the earth and the natural environment, in marked contrast to what Rachael Carson (1962) in *Silent Spring* called agriculture as an engineer would have it.

AGRICULTURE: A TAKEOVER THEORY

If women were doing so beautifully, why did they not continue to control agriculture as they had controlled horticulture? Why, as the dependence on cultivation steadily rose in any society did the participation of women cultivators decline?

---

[10] Three examples of axial rotation (turning motion around an axis) exist among primitive objects besides the vehicular wheel: the spindle whorl, the rotary quern, and the potter's wheel (Earl of Halsbury, 1971; p. 13)—all connected with women's work. As Halsbury notes, whichever came first certainly influenced the others. Also, as has often been noted, in Meso-America the wheel appeared only on children's toys (Doster *et al.*, 1978; p. 55), which were likely to have been made by women.

[11] The crank bends part of its axis at right angles to another part, which enables it to transform reciprocating motion (back and forth) to circular motion or vice versa, a vital step in the history of mechanics.

Agriculture, as defined by Murdock and White (1969, p. 353), is cultivation that uses irrigation, fertilization, crop rotation, or other techniques that largely eliminate fallowing. It is more extensive than horticulture, dealing in fields rather than gardens. Most often it involves cultivation with the plough rather than the hoe, although there are exceptions such as the Incas. The Agricultural Period begins about 3500 BC in the Middle East and a little later in the highlands near Tehuacán in Mexico.[12]

As horticulture develops into agriculture, people depend on cultivation for ever larger percentages of their diet. Simultaneously, another change occurs: a shift in the gender of the cultivator. Women become less and less likely to be the exclusive or primary cultivators. In a representative sample of 104 horticultural societies chosen by Martin and Voorhies (1975, p. 283), 50 per cent had exclusively female cultivators; another 33 per cent had shared cultivation, and only about 17 per cent had exclusively male cultivators. Among 93 agricultural societies, by contrast, only 16 per cent had exclusively female cultivators, 3 per cent shared cultivation, and 81 per cent had exclusively male cultivators. Indeed, the relationship between exclusive female cultivation and a group's dietary dependence on cultivation is almost directly inverse: some 67 per cent of societies depending on cultivation for 25 per cent of the diet or less have exclusively female cultivators. This percentage falls steadily as dependence rises, to a low of about 20 per cent exclusively female cultivators at 75 per cent dependence or above (Martin and Voorhies, 1975; p. 215). The shift from female to male cultivators, and with it presumably the primary role in technological innovation, has not been total. In areas of Africa, women still do 70 per cent of the agricultural work (Boulding, 1977; p. 119); in East Asia there are women who put in at least as many hours on farm work as men do.[13] There is historical evidence from both East Asia and Central America of significant agricultural inventions of women. In the nineteenth century patent records of both the United States and Britain, there is an impressive list of women inventors of agricultural machinery and devices, as well as innovators in research on plants. (See, for example, Bray, 1979, 1980; Mozans, 1913; Hanaford, 1882; James et al., 1971; Hyams, 1971; Stanley, 1982.) Soviet and Chinese women have been recognized for their contributions to plant research (Dodge, 1966; O'Neill, 1979).[14]

Yet woman as cultivator and inventor in cultivation becomes the exception rather than the rule as we move from horticulture to agriculture, and a society becomes increasingly dependent on cultivation for its diet. The question remains, Why?

Various theories have been advanced to explain the trend that culminated in male technological dominance of agriculture, especially in the West—a trend inextricably bound up with the development of male political dominance of society as a whole.[15] All of the explanations have merit. None of them, however, seems to answer the questions demanded of an adequate theory: not only how the plough, a distinguishing feature of agriculture, became a male preserve if it was first invented and used by women; but what made ploughing and other cultivative tasks—indeed, the whole cultivative role—attractive to men if previously

---

[12] About 2500–2300 BC.

[13] According to Francesca Bray (1980) of the East Asian History of Science Library, Cambridge, England, 'Although it is true that women don't usually drive the plough, they often contribute at least as much as the men in terms of (hours), as they are usually responsible for weeding, stone-picking, transplanting rice seedlings, play an equal part in harvesting, and are exclusively responsible for hulling, polishing, grinding, etc.'.

[14] This material on women inventors in agriculture is explored and documented in *Mothers of Invention* (Stanley, 1982).

[15] In horticultural societies, food is one of the main sources of power.

they had been content with hunting or herding or other economic roles?[16] What made women willing (or how could they be forced) to give up their main economic role, a role providing substantial and increasing status as the society depended more and more heavily on the food they produced,[17] especially where they also controlled food distribution?[18] In the Middle East, at least, agricultural surpluses were evidently stored in temples devoted to the Goddess and originally under the control of her priestesses (Stone, 1976; pp. 38, 40, 41).

How and why, then, did the sexual division of labor in cultivation change? In exploring reasons for the change, I shall draw examples mainly from the Middle East, a region from which much of Western cultural and institutional heritage derives. Although societal developments and influential variables have differed widely across cultures, it may be possible to propose a general theory that can be applied broadly with local variations.

Ester Boserup points out (Martin and Voorhies, 1975; pp. 278 ff.) that agriculture demands a greater total time investment than horticulture, especially in view of the rapid population increase that seems always to accompany the shift to agriculture and the settled life.[19] Women, then, already occupied with much of the other work of the society, and finding more hours needed for cultivation, might have begun to need help with their cultivative tasks.

But why did men take over the particular tasks they did? Much has been written about the male symbolism of the plough as it penetrates the earth for the insertion of the seed, and the fact that the Aryan terms for ploughs and seed-drills often derive from the words for penis, semen, etc. (Bray, private communication, 1980). Such a psychological basis for males' finding ploughing an appropriate role seems valid, especially if the timing ties in with the domestication of animals and the resulting certain knowledge of the male role in procreation. With the invention of animal-drawn ploughs, the tie-in might be even clearer wherever men herded and cared for the draft animals.[20] Ploughing can also be seen as an extension of land-clearing, a role that males sometimes took over even in horticultural societies.

Males may have invented the newer earth-turning ploughs (by 3500 BC the Egyptian variety already had an iron ploughshare; Partridge, 1973; p. 36), or such ploughs may have been introduced by trading contacts or by invaders. Although as mentioned above, women could certainly have wielded the early ploughs that they developed from hoes, and might have been able to handle the new ploughs as well if not weakened by causes not prevailing in early horticultural times (see below), it is true that the new ploughs required considerably more strength to force through the ground. If we see these new ploughs as the high technology of their era, and assume that for some or all of these reasons males operated them, we can locate one factor in the trend toward male dominance in agriculture.

---

[16] For example, Ester Boserup found contemporary male villagers very reluctant to leave hunting, fishing, or herding for either hoeing or ploughing (Martin and Voorhies, 1975; p. 279).

[17] Among the Iroquois, food was wealth. And when cultivation triumphed over hunting in Çatal Hüyük (fifty-eighth century BC), women gained in power (Martin and Voorhies, 1975; p. 226; Mellaart, cited in Rohrlich-Leavitt, 1977; p. 40).

[18] As, for example, among the Iroquois (Martin and Voorhies, 1975; pp. 225 ff.), where women were the exclusive cultivators. The women of each longhouse held a common store of food which they allocated to their men and children. Thus they controlled not only everyday life, but warfare, as the men did not hunt on raids, and had to petition the women for special supplies of dried food.

[19] The Enga of the New Guinea Highlands, for example, are supposed to have increased from 1146 to 100,000 people in only 300 years, after sweet potato cultivation and a settled lifestyle came to their lands (Watson, 1965; p. 302). Contrast this with humankind's previous record of 2–3 million years of zero population growth, or at least relatively stable populations, going back to *Homo erectus* (Boulding, 1976; p. 11).

[20] Interestingly enough, however, Athena is credited with inventing the ox yoke, and Ceres is credited with first taming oxen and accustoming them to the yoke (Grant, 1962; p. 89; Boccaccio, 1963; p. 11).

However, even where males took over ploughing, they could still be seen (and see themselves) as the women's helpers, and the women still in charge, much as men today speak of helping women with housework rather than sharing it. Perhaps more important than ploughing in the Middle East, is large-scale irrigation, another of the features often used to distinguish agriculture from horticulture. Women probably invented small-scale irrigation several times in several parts of the world during the horticultural period. Presumably, for example, it was female cultivators who led perennial spring waters to Jericho's grain and vegetable plots in 8000 BC (Hawkes, 1976; p. 40); Dayak women (Malaysia) build bamboo aqueducts (Mason, 1894; p. 25); and Ross (1896, p. 406) credits the Dayaks with 'a system of irrigation that would do credit to a far more civilized people'; New Guinea Highland cultivators (mostly women) irrigate with bamboo piping (Brookfield, 1961; p. 438). But the system that works for gardens may not work for the larger fields made necessary by larger populations; and again, women may have had too little time to get involved in 'the great system of canals that was to make all southern Mesopotamia fertile by 3000 BC' (Hawkes, 1976; p. 43). In any case, it has always been assumed, and I have found no proof to the contrary,[21] that males built and operated these far-flung engineering projects.

Even as horticulture is developing into agriculture, then, and as societies come to depend on cultivation for a major share of their diet, men seem to have taken control of two important technologies, ploughing and irrigation. Let us consider the newly emerging desirability of the cultivative role during the late Horticultural Period.

As the women of a society perfected their horticultural skills and tools, they would naturally have increased the productivity of their gardens. At some point, the men may have begun to feel that their hunting and fishing were no longer necessary or were losing status as less reliable than gardening. In societies where these were virtually their only economic roles, the sense of role loss could have been severe (cf. Boulding, 1976; p. 149). At the very least we can hypothesize that emergent agricultural societies would see the cultivative role as important and increasingly desirable. Several courses seem open to men in such a situation: they can elevate hunting to a religion or near religion and continue with it as their main or only economic role; they can transform hunting into herding and make their own contribution to the food supply more reliable; they can transform hunting into warfare and go on raiding parties instead of hunting parties; they can begin to participate in the newly desirable role of cultivator wherever possible; or they can work out some combination of these. In the middle East and other cultures more directly antecedent to our own, men seem to have chosen cultivation with some archaic survival of the religion and warfare roles.

If the cultivative role was indeed so desirable, why do women give it up, or give up important parts of it? The domestication of animals may have played a significant part. Even where men did the herding, women often had to milk those animals used for milk, then process and store the milk and milk products. In addition, the care of smaller domesticated

---

[21] The semi-mythical Semiramis, who lived later than the beginnings of large-scale irrigation (ninth century BC) and whose accomplishments may reflect those of other noblewomen of the same name living at different times, is credited variously with inventing canals, bridges over rivers, causeways over swamps, the chastity belt (to keep a courtesan from gaining influence over her son); the caftan; war engines that ended a siege; and the Hanging Gardens of Babylon, where the first irrigation by sprinkling supposedly took place. She is also supposed to have devised a way to strengthen a tunnel over the Euphrates, and Herodotus credits her with the bank containing the Euphrates (Boccaccio, fourteenth century (1963); pp. 6–7; Gage, 1870; pp. 22–23; Mozans, 1976; p. 346; *Encyclopaedia Britannica*, 11th edn.; Fukuda, 1976; pp. 21–22).

animals as dogs, chickens, and pigs usually fell to women, increasing their already heavy workload still further. The domestication of animals also made unmistakable the male role in procreation, a development that could undermine women's exclusive responsibility for fertility at a crucial time.

Another factor—probably the most important—is a population explosion. Chroniclers duly note the rapid expansion of population that invariably follows the introduction of agriculture. But often ignored is the *direct impact of a population explosion on women, and the actual mechanism of that explosion.* For a graphic example of both, consider the case of the foraging !Kung of Angola, Botswana, and Southwest Africa, who have very recently been settled into villages and shifted to a grain-based diet (Kolata, 1978, and Draper, 1975, *passim*). Among the foraging !Kung the two sexes are roughly equal in status, with the women contributing 60–80 per cent of the group's food by weight. Among the settled groups, however, women are losing their egalitarian status, and the birth rate has risen 30 per cent in only 5 years!

Here we can observe firsthand a development that is usually lost in the past and that may have taken hundreds or even thousands of years elsewhere. In less than a decade the !Kung women seem to be losing status partly because they no longer contribute significantly to the food supply (men leave the village to farm and herd Bantu cattle for wages), partly because they have lost mobility (women stay home and care for houses and children), and partly because their men are starting to imitate the neighboring male-dominated Bantu. Contributing to women's loss of mobility (which will aggravate their loss of status as their men learn the Bantu language and move faster into modernity) is their higher fertility. In the nomadic state, mostly because of a less rich diet,[22] puberty came late (15.5 years). Women had their first child at about 19.5 years, and had babies only about every 4 years thereafter (Kolata, 1978; p. 121)—partly because they nursed the infants for 3–4 years and thus had too little body fat to ovulate during that time. Now puberty comes earlier, and the interval between births has dropped 30 per cent. Women stop nursing sooner and supplement their babies' diets with cow's milk and grains. Their own diets being richer, they ovulate regularly and have babies much more often, with marked effects on mobility and division of labor.

The greater number of children has another, more subtle effect on the status of women. Among the nomadic !Kung there were so few children that all ages and both sexes played together. This kind of playgrouping discourages the development of distinct games and roles for the two sexes (Draper, 1975; p. 89; Kolata, 1978; p. 120). Now, with more children, and with boys going off with their fathers to herd cattle, this equalizing effect is lost.

Anthropologist Shirley Lee (1966) has observed the same sort of changes among the settled as opposed to the nomadic Paiutes. Excessive childbearing puts women at a physical disadvantage in three ways: it produces more periods of very early and very late pregnancy, which can be dangerous for heavy work (such as ploughing); (b) the care of several young children is more exhausting both emotionally and physically than the care of one; and (c) prolonged excessive childbearing will eventually undermine the health. A woman thus overburdened, with all her other tasks increased or continuing unabated, is in no position to reflect on the future political consequences if a man offers to clear the land for her garden or do her ploughing.

---

[22] Less rich, but actually better. Low in fat and nearly salt-free, the !Kung foraging diet keeps its people free from circulatory disease for the most part. It exceeds UN recommendations for people of their stature, and is much higher in protein than the typical African diet (Shostak, 1977; pp. 46–47).

Wherever patriliny and patri- or neolocal residence replaced matriliny and matrilocal residence, women's power, self-esteem, and status would have declined further, another factor weakening women's resistance to a male takeover of their food cultivator role. Moreover, this development could have compounded the effect of the population explosion, as women would no longer have had their mothers and sisters at hand to share the child-care burdens. This shift in descent and residence patterns, by interrupting the traditional mother–daughter continuity, may also have interrupted traditional instruction in contraception and abortion.[23]

A final factor for the Middle East—and for nineteenth and twentieth century Africa—is the political and religious invasion by patriarchal and male-dominated peoples that took place beginning about 2500 BC (Stone, 1976; Ch. 1, 3–5). This factor needs further evaluation, but the dates of the invasion coincide remarkably well with certain landmark dates for women's loss of status in Crete and Sumer and throughout the Middle East (Rohrlich-Leavitt, 1977, *passim*; Stone, 1976; Ch. 3). The invasion is relevant here for several reasons: the invaders deliberately set about undermining the status of women, primary devotees and beneficiaries of the local Goddess religions, in order to introduce their own male god. Both the attack and its eventual success would further weaken women's ability to resist a takeover of their role in cultivation—as of their general role in society. Moreover, agricultural surpluses, which were stored in the temples for redistribution in times of need and originally under control of the priestesses, would have passed to control of the priests after the victory of patriarchal religion. Finally, since agriculture was itself an important part of the Goddess religion—not just woman's work and a woman's economic role, but a woman's mystery (Graves, 1955; vol. I, p. 93)—an attack on that religion could scarcely avoid an attack on woman's dominance in agriculture.[24]

Preoccupied and possibly weakened, then, by more frequent childbearing, excluded from some of the latest agricultural technology (the deep plough and large-scale irrigation), deprived perhaps of matrilineal support networks and eventually of the ego-support and power of the Goddess religion, women may have been less able to resist a takeover of their cultivative role just at a time when men, feeling deprived of a meaningful role in hunting, saw a chance for power. Considering division of labor alone, if cultivation began to demand significantly more time just as women's childbearing and -rearing role also mushroomed, men may have been the only ones free to give that time. Thus women agriculturalists in many areas entered the shadows of a long dark age from which they have yet to emerge.[25]

---

[23] When women have no mothers or sisters to share childcare burdens, they draft their daughters, depriving girl children of mobility and freedom to explore and the chance to learn any other economic or social role. Instruction in contraception and abortion traditionally occurred either at puberty from the mother or in a formal initiation rite, or after childbirth, the midwife giving guidance particularly after the birth of the number of children thought desirable in the society (Himes, 1936). The women's network of birth-control lore could be broken when a girl left home before puberty and then gave birth among her husband's kin where the midwife owed allegiance to his family and not to hers.

[24] Clearly, women resisted the agricultural takeover. According to Robert Graves' summary of Demeter's nature and deeds (1955, I:89–96), Demeter had a 'gentle soul', and dealt harshly with very few men. One of those few was Erysichthon, whom she punished with insatiable hunger for daring to enter one of her sacred groves and cut down trees. The usual punishment for that crime was death. Moreover, Erysichthon's name means earth-tearer. Thus his real crime was probably daring to plough without Demeter's consent. There were taboos against men's ploughing, planting grain, and especially against planting beans, for beans were symbollically connected with ghosts or souls.

[25] Lest this be thought a biology-is-destiny theory, I emphasize once again that the 'natural' state of affairs is probably much more closely represented by the millions of years during which human and proto-human populations remained stable, up to about 10,000 BC; and that we are dealing here not so much with biology as with biology run amok on a grain-rich diet.

REFERENCES

An ancient people's antibiotic. 1980. *San Francisco Chronicle* 26 Sept. p. 11.

Boccaccio, Giovanni. Fourteenth century (1963). *Of Famous Women*, Guarino, Guido A. (trans.). Rutgers University Press, New Brunswick, New Jersey.

Boulding, Elise. 1976. *The Underside of History*. Westview Press, Boulder, Colorado.

Boulding, Elise. 1977. *Women in the Twentieth Century World*. Wiley, New York.

Bray, Francesca. 1979, 1980. East Asian History of Science Library, Cambridge, England. Interview, 30 May 1979; personal communications, 1980.

British Broadcasting Company. 1979. 'Tomorrow's World' Program, 31 May, BBC 1 TV.

Brookfield, H. C. 1961. The Highland peoples of New Guinea. *Geographical Journal* **127**, 437 ff.

Carson, Rachel. 1962. *The Silent Spring*. Houghton Mifflin, Boston.

Chapple, Eliot D. and Coon, Carleton S. 1942. *Principles of Anthropology*. Holt, New York.

Davis, Elizabeth Gould. 1971. *The First Sex*. Putnam, New York.

Dodge, Norton T. 1966. *Women in the Soviet Economy*. Johns Hopkins University Press, Baltimore, Maryland.

Draper, Patricia. 1975. !Kung women: contrasts in sexual egalitarianism in foraging and sedentary contexts. In: Reiter, Rayna ed. *Toward an Anthropology of Women*, pp. 77–109. Monthly Review Press, New York.

Frazer, Sir James George. 1930. *Myths on the Origin of Fire*. Macmillan, London.

Fukuda, Hitoshi. 1976. *Irrigation in the World: Comparative Developments*. University of Tokyo Press, Tokyo.

Gage, Matilda Joslyn. 1870. *Woman as Inventor*. New York State Woman Suffrage Association, Fayetteville, New York.

Grant, Michael. 1962. *Myths of the Greeks and Romans*. World Publishing, Cleveland, Ohio.

Graves, Robert. 1955. *The Greek Myths*, 2 vols. Penguin Books, Baltimore, Maryland.

Halsbury, Earl of. 1971. Invention and technological progress, 4th Annual Spooner Lecture. *The Inventor* (London), pp. 10–34, June.

Hanaford, Phebe A. 1882. *Daughters of America*, 2nd edn. True, Augusta, Maine.

Hawkes, Jacquetta. 1976. *The Atlas of Early Man*. St. Martins, New York.

Himes, Norman E. 1936. *Medical History of Contraception*. Shocken, New York.

Hyams, Edward. 1971. *A History of Gardens and Gardening*. Praeger. New York.

James, Edward T., *et al.* 1971. *Notable American Women 1607–1950: A Biographical Dictionary*, 3 vols. Harvard University Press, Cambridge, Massachusetts.

Kolata, Gina B. 1978. !Kung hunter-gatherers: feminism, diet, and birth control. In: Logan, Michael H. and Hunt, Edward E., Jr. eds. *Health and the Human Condition*. Duxbury Press, North Scituate, Massachusetts.

Kroeber, Theodora. 1964. *Ishi, Last of His Tribe*. Parnassus Press, Berkeley, California.

Lee, Richard B. and DeVore, Irven, eds. 1968. *Man the Hunter*. Aldine Publishing, Chicago.

Lee, Shirley. 1966. A survey of acculturation in the Intermontane area of the United States. MA Thesis, Dept. of Anthropology, Stanford University, California.

Martin, M. Kay and Voorhies, Barbara. 1975. *Female of the Species*. Columbia University Press, New York.

Mason, Otis T. 1894. *Woman's Share in Primitive Culture*. Appleton, New York.

Mason, Otis T. 1895 (1902). *The Origins of Invention*. London (Scribner's, New York).

Mellaart, James. 1965. Çatal Hüyük, a neolithic city in Anatolia. *Proc. Br. R. Acad.* **51**, 201 ff.

Mellaart, James. 1973. *The Neolithic of the Near East*. Scribner's, New York.

Mozans, H. J. 1913 (1976). *Woman in Science*. Appleton, New York (MIT Press, Cambridge, Massachusetts).

Murdock, George P. and White, Douglas R. 1969. Standard cross-cultural sample. *Ethnology* **8** (4), 329–369.

Murdock, George P. and Provost, Caterina. 1973. Factors in the division of labor by sex. *Ethnology* **12** (2), 203–225.

Murphy, Yolanda and Murphy, Robert. 1974. *Women of the Forest*. Columbia University Press, New York.

O'Neill, Lois D. 1979. *The Woman's Book of World Records and Achievements*. Doubleday, New York.

Partridge, Michael. 1973. *Farm Tools Through the Ages*. Osprey, Reading, England.

Reed, Evelyn. 1975. *Woman's Evolution: From Matriarchal Clan to Patriarchal Family*. Pathfinder, New York.

Rohrlich-Leavitt, Ruby. 1977. Women in transition: Crete and Sumer. In: Bridenthal, Renate and Koonz, Claudia eds. *Becoming Visible*, pp. 36–59. Houghton Mifflin, Boston.

Ross, H. Ling. 1896. *Natives of Sarawak and British North Borneo*. Truslove, New York.

Shostak, Marjorie. 1977. Life before horticulture. *Horticulture* **55**, 38 ff.

Sokolov, Raymond. 1978. Root awakening. *Natural History* **87** (9), 34 ff.

Spretnak, Charlene. 1978. *Lost Goddesses of Early Greece: A Collection of Pre-Hellenic Mythology*. Moon Books, Berkeley, California.

Stanley, Autumn. 1982. *Mothers of Invention*. Scarecrow, Metuchen, NJ.

Stone, Merlin. 1976. *When God Was a Woman*. Harcourt, Brace, New York.

Tanner, Nancy and Zihlmann, Adrienne. 1976. Women in evolution, part I: innovation and selection in human origins. *Signs* **1** (3), 585–608.

Triplett, Glover B., Jr. and Van Doren, David M., Jr. 1977. Agriculture without tillage. *Scientific American* Jan., 28 ff.

Vietmayer, Noel. 1979. The greening of the future. *Quest/79*, Sept., 25 ff.

Watson, James B. 1965. From hunting to horticulture in the New Guinea highlands. *Ethnology* **4** (3) 295–309.
White, Lynn, Jr. 1978. *Medieval Religion and Technology*. University of California Press, Berkeley, California.
Zihlmann, Adrienne. 1978. Women in evolution, part II: subsistence and social organization among early hominids. *Signs* **4** (1), 4–20.

Women's Studies Int. Quart., Vol. 4, No. 3, pp. 305–312, 1981.
Printed in Great Britain.

0148–0685/81/030305–08$02.00/0
Pergamon Press Ltd.

WOMEN AND TECHNOLOGY IN ANCIENT ALEXANDRIA: MARIA AND HYPATIA

MARGARET ALIC

2380 SW Osage, Portland OR 97205, U.S.A.

Synopsis—Since earliest times women have been important contributors to the advancement of technology, but we know very little about the work of specific women in antiquity. This paper reviews our knowledge of the technological innovations made by two women in Alexandria—Maria the Jewess and Hypatia. Their inventions may be the earliest technological work that can be ascribed to individual women. Maria probably lived in the first century. She was one of the founders of both theoretical and experimental alchemy. She is credited with the invention of laboratory apparatus that remain basic tools of the modern chemist. Hypatia (370–415) is better known for her mathematical work, but her designs for scientific instruments are of interest as examples of the technological work of ancient women. Her death marked the end of Greek science.

'There have been very learned women as there have been women warriors, but there have never been women inventors' (Voltaire, 1764).

Voltaire was wrong. Since the earliest times women have not only been inventors, but often they have been at the forefront of technological innovation. The names and circumstances of many of these women are lost. But in the great Hellenic city of Alexandria in the first centuries of the Christian era, two women—Maria and Hypatia—achieved a renown for their designs for scientific instruments.

ALEXANDRIAN SCIENCE

The city of Alexandria was founded at the mouth of the Nile River by Alexander the Great in the fourth century BC. In 306 BC Alexander's general Ptolemy took over the rule of Egypt and established the Ptolemaic dynasty with its capital at Alexandria. The city quickly grew into a cosmopolitan metropolis of Egyptians, Greeks and Jews, with a population approaching one million (Partington, 1970). Like Alexander, Ptolemy had been a pupil of Aristotle and he founded the Alexandrian Museum, an institution modelled on Aristotle's Lyceum and devoted to teaching and research. At its height, 100 professors staffed the Museum, their salaries paid by the State. It boasted the Great Library, a zoo, botanical gardens, an astronomical observatory and dissecting rooms (Mason, 1962). Within a matter of years Alexandria had become not only a major center of trade for the Greek and Arab Worlds, but had replaced Athens as the center of Greek science. Philosophers, scientists and intellectuals were attracted to Alexandria by the scholarly climate and liberal funds. In the third and second centuries BC Alexandria was the home of some of the greatest scientists of antiquity. It was also the center for the development of practical technology. When Egypt succumbed to the Romans in 30 BC, Alexandria became the intellectual hub of the Empire.

By the second century AD the Greco-Roman world had entered a period of intellectual and scientific decline. All important knowledge was thought to reside in the work of the 'ancients' (the classical Greeks). Even Claudius Ptolemy (AD 85–165), one of the most important observational astronomers of antiquity, could barely conceive of himself or his contemporaries formulating new ideas or making discoveries unknown to their predecessors (Hall and Hall, 1964). The Roman rulers had scant interest in science and the intellectual society of Alexandria became increasingly divided among the pagans, Jews and Christians.

Alchemy was the one science which flourished in Alexandria in these barren times. The early alchemists were the first practitioners of experimental science. The antecedents of Alexandrian alchemy can be found in ancient Mesopotamia, where women were developing the chemical processes of distillation, extraction and sublimation for use in the formulation of perfumes and cosmetics. Along with the manufacture of imitation jewelry, these crafts later became major Egyptian industries. The apparatus and recipes utilized by Babylonian women chemists were similar to those used in cooking.[1] In first century Alexandrian women scientists combined the theoretical foundations of alchemy with the chemistry of the craft traditions.

MARIA THE ALCHEMIST

Alchemy is usually defined as the search for the processes that produce the elixir of longevity and transmute common metals into gold. It was a strange and secret science, a combination of mystical rituals and laboratory experimentation. Historians often dismiss it as incomprehensible sorcery, but the alchemists of antiquity were seeking to understand the nature of process and of life. Grounded in Aristotelian science, they were the first to combine theory with experimentation. Early Egyptian alchemy distinguished between the mystical and the practical. The alchemical papyri contained recipes for simulating gold and silver using alloys of other metals or by gilding the surface of a base metal. In the technical recipes the products were seen as imitations, while in the mystical works they were described as true transmutations (Mason, 1962). Metals were thought to be living organisms evolving toward the perfection of gold, and the alchemist was simply encouraging the natural process by transferring the spirit or vapor of gold to a base metal, as manifested by the transfer of color (Hopkins, 1925).

Secrecy was the cornerstone of alchemy and the writings were often published under the name of an ancient deity or celebrity, either for the protection of the alchemist or to promote acceptance of her work. One of the earliest alchemical treatises was ascribed to the goddess Isis and she became known as the founder of the arcane science.

Likewise Maria the Jewess wrote under the name of Miriam the Prophetess, sister of Moses, causing some historians to mistakenly identify the biblical Miriam as an alchemist.[2] Maria is thought to have lived and worked in Alexandria in the first century, although she is occasionally placed as late as the third century. She was said to have written many books which were later expanded on, corrupted and confused with other works (Burland, 1968).

---

[1] Levey, Martin. 1956. Babylonian chemistry. *Osiris* **12**, 376–389. Levey discusses the importance of women in the development of early chemical techniques and supplies the names of two women perfumers mentioned in Babylonian cuneiform texts. Women were also instrumental in the development of Chinese alchemy.

[2] Maria is referred to in the literature by a variety of names and epithets including Mary or Maria Prophetissa, 'Maria the Sage' and Miriam.

None of her writings are extant, but fragments exist, quoted in the works of other early alchemists, particularly those of the Egyptian encyclopediast Zosimos (AD 300).[3]

Maria's alchemical theories were to prove influential, but her most significant contributions were inventions and designs for laboratory apparatus. These she described clearly and in great detail, judging from the quotes preserved in the writings of Zosimos (Taylor, 1949). Maria's water bath or *Balneum mariae* has remained an essential piece of laboratory equipment for nearly 2000 years. 'Maria's bath' resembled a double boiler and was used, as is a modern water bath, to slowly heat a substance or to maintain it at a constant temperature. In modern French a double boiler is still called a *bain marie*.

Maria is thought to have invented a still or alembic. It consisted of a furnace, an earthenware vessel (*the bikos*) for holding the liquid to be distilled, a copper or bronze tube or still-head (the *ambix*) for condensing the vapor, a delivery spout (the *solen*) fitted into the still-head, and a receiving vessel. She described how to make the copper tubing from sheet metal and compared the thickness of the tubes with a 'pastry cook's copper frying pan' (Taylor, 1949; p. 39). Flour paste was recommended for luting the joints. She also invented the *tribikos*, a still with three copper or bronze delivery spouts, each 'about a cubit and a half' in length, for separating distillates (Fig. 1).[4]

The *kerotakis* was the triangular palette on which ancient painters heated their mixtures of wax and pigment. Maria used the same palette for softening metals and impregnating them with colors and *kerotakis* came to signify her entire reflux apparatus. It consisted of a closed sphere or cylinder with a pan near the bottom containing sulfur or mercury. Near the top of the cylinder was the metal palette (the *kerotakis* proper) containing a copper–lead alloy or some other metal to be treated. The entire apparatus sat on a fire and was closed at the top with a hemispherical cover (Fig. 2). The heat vaporized the sulfur or mercury. The vapor

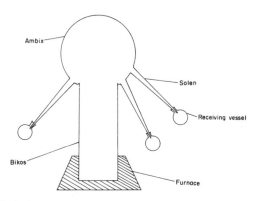

Fig. 1. F. Sherwood Taylor's reconstruction of the *Tribikos* or three-armed still (Drawing by Debbie Lev).

---

[3] Zosimos, a disciple of Maria, worked in collaboration with his sister Theosebeia.

[4] Maria's still is illustrated in 'The Gold-making of Kleopatra' a page of diagrams from the third-century 'Leiden' papyrus and attributed to a woman alchemist named Kleopatra Chrisopoeia. This is one of the oldest of alchemical documents. Kleopatra was associated with Maria's school and may have been her contemporary in Alexandria. Primarily known for the allegorical poetry of her alchemical *Dialogue*, Kleopatra was also the author of a work on weights and measures. (Lindsay, Jack. 1970. *The Origins of Alchemy in Graeco-Roman Egypt.* Barnes & Noble, New York.) Kleopatra is often confused with the Egyptian queen who also may have been interested in alchemy. Kleopatra's writings may have been deliberately ascribed to the infamous Queen Cleopatra.

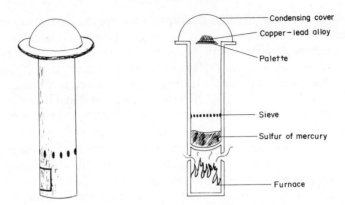

FIG. 2. F. Sherwood Taylor's reconstruction of the *kerotakis* (Drawing by Debbie Lev).

condensed at the top of the cylinder, the liquid flowing back to the bottom, thereby establishing a continuous reflux. Sulfur vapors acted on the copper–lead alloy yielding a black substance—'Mary's Black'—thought to represent the first stage of transmutation. Other metals and vapors gave different products (Holmyard, 1968). The *kerotakis* was also used for the extraction of plant oils such as the perfume attar of roses (Federmann, 1969). Maria also invented or improved upon the hot-ash bath and the dung-bed as heat sources and she perfected processes for making gems phosphoresce (Lindsay, 1970).

Maria made many contributions to alchemical theory, particularly on the nature of color and the sexual conjugation of metals. She believed that metals were living beings, male or female. The laboratory products of the alchemist were the result of sexual generation: 'Unite the male with the female, and you will find what you seek' (Mason, 1962; p. 67). She applied the ancient concept of the macrocosm and the microcosm to the 'above–below' arrangement in distillation and reflux (Lindsay, 1970).

In the third century the Roman emperor Diocletian began the persecution of Alexandrian alchemists and the suppression of their work. This marked the demise of alchemy as a true experimental science. But Maria's influence continued to be felt. The Arabs adopted the theories of the Alexandrian adepts and they venerated Maria. Her work reached the West via Arab translations during the Middle Ages, but by that time alchemy had degenerated into mystical mumbo-jumbo. There were few advances in laboratory chemistry from the fall of Alexandria until the middle of the seventeenth century, and the techniques and apparatus developed by Maria the Jewess still serve as basic tools of the laboratory chemist.

THE INVENTIONS OF HYPATIA

The scientific life of Alexandria declined steadily after the first century AD. A slight renaissance occurred in the fourth century, but it was marked by a plateau in the decline rather than by any major scientific or technological advance. But this fourth-century renaissance was illuminated by Hypatia—the most famous woman scientist in antiquity.

Many writers have romanticized the life and death of Hypatia, ignoring her scientific achievements and capitalizing on her tragic demise.[5] To feminists she has come to represent the plight of the woman scholar and for historians she often symbolizes the end of ancient science. The last of the pagan scientists, her violent death coincided with the last years of the Roman Empire, and after Hypatia, there were no significant advances in mathematics, astronomy or physics anywhere in the West for another 1000 years. Though the intellectual recession had been in progress for several centuries prior to Hypatia, after her came only the chaos and barbarism of the Dark Ages.

When Hypatia was born in 370, the intellectual life of Alexandria was already in a state of dangerous confusion. The Roman Empire was converting and more often than not the Christian zealot saw only heresy and evil magic in mathematics and science. The Second Coming was imminent, so the Christian world had no need for technological advance. The Romans burned the Great Library. In 389, when Hypatia was nineteen, the Serapeum Library was sacked in a Christian riot by order of Theophilos, Bishop of Alexandria. It was not a propitious era in which to become a scientist.

Hypatia's father, Theon, was a mathematician and astronomer and later, director of the University. He closely supervised every aspect of his daughter's physical and academic education. According to legend he was determined that she develop into a 'perfect human being'—this in an age when females were often considered to be less than human!

After travelling abroad for several years, Hypatia was offered the chair of mathematics and philosophy at the University of Alexandria. She became one of the school's most popular teachers. Students converged on the city to attend her lectures on maths, astronomy, philosophy and mechanics, and her home became an intellectual center for students and scholars. Most of her writings originated as texts for her students (Osen, 1974). Although none of them have survived intact, there are numerous references to her works.

Hypatia was a Neo-Platonist. Although she may have studied at the mystical Neo-Platonic school of Plutarch the Younger and his daughter Asclepigenia in Athens (Mozans, 1913), she subscribed to the more scholarly and scientific branch of Neo-Platonism founded at the Museum by Plotinus in the third century. No matter. To the Christians all Neo-Platonists were dangerous heretics.

Hypatia was primarily an algebraist and she wrote a commentary on the *Arithmetica* of Diophantus, some of which was subsequently incorporated into the diophantine manuscripts (Heath, 1964). She authored a popularization of the *Conics of Apollonius* and it is likely that she assisted her father in his revision of Euclid's *Elements*—the edition that is still in use today. Hypatia and Theon collaborated on at least one treatise on Euclid and on a commentary on Ptolemy's astronomical canon, the *Almagest* (Rizzo, 1954).

Hypatia was also interested in mechanics and practical technology. Information on this aspect of her work comes from the extant letters of her student and friend Synesius of Cyrene, who went on to become the wealthy and powerful Bishop of Ptolemais. These letters contain Hypatia's designs for several scientific instruments. Among them are directions for constructing an astrolabe, a device probably first invented by Hipparchus (*ca.* 150 BC). Hypatia's astrolabe probably looked something like this: the body or mater was a thick metal

---

[5] Kingsley, Charles. 1853. *Hypatia*. Conkley, Chicago. Hubbard, Elbert. 1928. *Little Journeys to the Homes of Great Teachers* Vol. 10, pp. 269–292. William Wise, New York. In his novel, Kingsley kills Hypatia off at age 25 instead of 45, so she hardly had a chance to do any scientific work. Hubbard's portrayal of her is fanciful and sarcastic. He claims that at age 20, Hypatia was 5 ft 9 in. tall, weighed 135 lb, had a 'flute-like' voice and 'a body of rarest grace' (p. 274). It is not known from what long-lost source Hubbard unearthed these statistics. He also contends that she hypnotized her students.

plate holding two rotating discs. The lower disc or plate had an engraved grid illustrating the visible horizon, the zenith, and the reference altitude and azimuth lines for an observer at a given latitude. Other plates could be substituted for different latitudes. The upper disc was an openwork metal plate, the rete or star map, representing the celestial sphere. Pointers indicated the positions of the brightest fixed stars and circles represented the zodiac and the ecliptic, the apparent path of the sun. The instrument was fastened with a removable peg running through the center of the discs (Fig. 3). The simplest plane astrolabe functioned as a star chart. Rotating the rete simulated the daily rotation of the celestial sphere. Primarily an instrument for calculations, by the time of Hypatia the astrolabe had been improved to the point where it could be used to work out many problems in spherical astronomy. It was used for calculating time and the ascending sign of the zodiac and for measuring the positions of stars, planets and the sun (Price, 1957).

Hypatia also developed an apparatus for distilling water, an instrument for measuring water level, and a graduated 'hydroscope' or hydrometer for determining the specific gravity of a liquid. This instrument, based on the work of Archimedes, was probably a sealed tube about the size of a flute and weighted at one end (Mozans, 1913). It sunk to a depth dependent on the specific gravity of a liquid.

FIG. 3(a). An early plane astrolabe (Drawing by Debbie Lev).

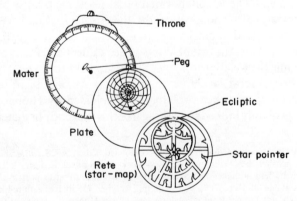

FIG. 3(b). The components of a plane astrolabe (Drawing by Debbie Lev).

THE END OF ANCIENT SCIENCE

Hypatia seems to have become enmeshed in Alexandrian politics. Her student Hesychius the Jew wrote:

'Donning the philosopher's cloak, and making her way through the midst of the city, she explained publicly the writings of Plato, or Aristotle, or any other philosopher, to all who wished to hear.... The magistrates were wont to consult her first in their administration of the affairs of the city' (McCabe, 1903; p. 269).

Hypatia was a scholarly pagan and a woman, an espouser of Greek scientific rationalism and an influential political figure. This proved to be a dangerous combination. A power struggle was developing between Cyril, who became patriarch of Alexandria in 412, and Hypatia's friend Orestes, the Roman prefect of Egypt. Hypatia was caught in the middle when Cyril began a systematic persecution of the 'heretical' Neo-Platonists at the University.

The account of the murder of Hypatia comes down to us in the fifth-century writings of Socrates Scholasticus (Freemantle, 1953):

'All men did both reverence and had her in admiration for the singular modesty of her mind. Wherefore she had great spite and envy owed unto her, and because she conferred oft, and had great familiarity with Orestes, the people charged her that she was the cause why the bishop and Orestes were not become friends. To be short, certain heady and rash cockbrains whose guide and captain was Peter, a reader of that Church, watched this woman coming from some place or other, they pull her out of her chariot: they haul her into the Church called Caesarium: they stripped her stark naked: they raze the skin and rend the flesh of her body with sharp shells, until the breath departed out of her body: they quarter her body: they bring her quarters unto a place called Cinaron and burn them to ashes'.

This crime took place in March 415, Hypatia's murderers were Parabolans, fanatical monks of the Church of St. Cyril of Jerusalem, possibly aided by Nitrian monks. Whether Cyril directly ordered the murder remains an open question. At the very least he created the political climate that made such an atrocity possible. Cyril was later canonized.

Orestes reported the murder and asked Rome to launch an investigation. He then resigned his office and fled Alexandria. The investigation was repeatedly postponed for 'lack of witnesses' and eventually Cyril put out the word that Hypatia was alive and well in Athens (Osen, 1974).

Hypatia's brutal murder marked the end of Platonic teachings in Alexandria and throughout the Roman Empire. In 581 the church declared that women had neither souls nor reason. With the spread of Christianity, the appearance of numerous religious cults and widespread political chaos, interest in astrology and mysticism replaced scientific research. In 640 Alexandria was invaded by the Arabs and all vestiges of the Museum destroyed. Europe had entered the Dark Ages.

REFERENCES

Burland, C. A. 1968. *The Arts of the Alchemists*. Macmillan, New York.
Federmann, Reinhard. 1969. *The Royal Art of Alchemy*. (Weber, Richard H. trans.). Chilton, Philadelphia.
Hall, A. Rupert and Hall, Marie Boas. 1964. *A Brief History of Science*. New American Library, New York.
Heath, Thomas L. 1964. *Diophantus of Alexandria: A Study on the History of Greek Algebra*. Dover, New York.

Holmyard, E. J. 1968. *Alchemy*. Penguin, Middlesex.

Hopkins, Arthur J. 1925. A modern theory of alchemy. *Isis* **7**, 58–76.

Hubbard, Elbert. 1928. *Little Journeys to the Homes of Great Teachers*. Vol. 10, pp. 269–292. William Wise, New York.

Kingsley, Charles. 1853. *Hypatia or New Foes with Old Faces*. Conkley, Chicago.

Levey, Martin. 1956. Babylonian chemistry: a study of Arabic and second millenium BC perfumery. *Osiris* **12**, 376–389.

Lindsay, Jack. 1970. *The Origins of Alchemy in Graeco-Roman Egypt*. Barnes & Noble, New York.

Mason, Stephen F. 1962. *A History of the Sciences* (rev. edn). Collier, New York.

McCabe, Joseph. 1903. Hypatia. *Critic* **43**, 267–272.

Mozans, H. J. (John Augustine Zahm). 1913. *Woman in Science*. Appleton, New York.

Osen, Lynn M. 1974. *Women in Mathematics*. MIT Press, Cambridge.

Partington, James R. 1970. *A History of Chemistry* Vol. 1, Part 1. Macmillan, London.

Price, Derek J. 1957. Precision instruments to 1500. In: Singer, Charles., Holmyard, E. J., Hall, A. R. and Williams, Trevor I. eds. *From the Renaissance to the Industrial Revolution*, Vol. III of *A History of Technology*, pp. 582–619. Clarendon, Oxford.

Rizzo, P. V. 1954. Early daughters of Urania. *Sky and Telescope* **14**, 7–10.

Socrates Scholasticus. Fifth century (1953). The murder of Hypatia. In: Freemantle, Ann ed. *A Treasury of Early Christianity*, pp. 379–380. Viking, New York.

Taylor, F. Sherwood. 1949. *The Alchemists: Founders of Modern Chemistry*. Schuman, New York.

Voltaire. 1764 (1901). Women. In: *Philosophical Dictionary* Vol. 10. Dumont, Paris.

Women's Studies Int. Quart., Vol. 4, No. 3, pp. 313–319, 1981.
Printed in Great Britain.

0148–0685/81/030313–07$02.00/0
Pergamon Press Ltd.

THE MACHINE IN UTOPIA: SHAKER WOMEN AND TECHNOLOGY

HELEN DEISS IRVIN

Transylvania University, Lexington, KY 40508, U.S.A.

Synopsis—Commonly believed devoted to handcrafts and opposed to technology, the nineteenth-century American Shakers were enthusiastic about the machine, viewing it as a means to a more humane life. Shaker women used, maintained, and even invented labor-saving devices, both in their domestic work and their commercial enterprises. The Shaker view toward women and technology emerged from their egalitarian religious principles that placed an equal value upon the lives of women and men. Shaker women invented the buzz saw, cut nails, and a successful revolving oven, and they were knowledgeable about the operation of machinery. Although they worked long hours at their machines, Shaker women emphasized that their lot was far better than that of unfortunate factory women, because they worked for themselves in pleasant surroundings and rotated work assignments frequently. Hard-working, they decried drudgery, and though they opposed capitalism and the factory system, they maintained a Utopian vision of technology as a source of a better American life.

Celebrated for their simple handcrafts, the Shakers of nineteenth-century America are widely considered isolated and primitive people who eschewed the developing technology of their era.[1] As Thomas Merton observes: 'Shaker craftsmanship is perhaps the last great expression of work in a purely human measure, a witness to the ancient, primitive, perfect totality of man before the final victory of machine technology' (Merton, 1966; p. xv).[2] But far from rejecting the machine, the Shakers envisioned technology as a means to a more humane life. Grinding labor, they believed, was not the inevitable lot of man, nor for that matter, of woman. For unlike women of some religious Utopias, such as the Amish, Shaker women did not view

---

[1] The United Society of Believers—the Shakers of 'Shaking Quakers'—originated in England about 1747 but did not flourish until a small group migrated to America in 1774. Harshly persecuted at first as British spies, the Shakers nonetheless attracted followers, and from their original settlement in Watervliet, New York, they gradually established thriving new communities in New York, Massachusetts, Connecticut, New Hampshire, and Maine, and as far west as Ohio and Kentucky. Celibate, they hoped to increase their number through conversion, but after the Civil War, they slowly declined, and their entire membership never exceeded 20,000 during the century. Suspected not only for their celibacy but also for their pacifism, their communism, and the shaking dances that accompanied their religious services, the Shakers earned respect for their hard work and striking material success. A few Shakers remain at Canterbury, New Hampshire, and Sabbathday Lake, Maine. Today interest in the Shakers is high in the United States, where exhibits of Shaker artifacts are popular and historical groups have restored entire Shaker villages.

[2] Scores of articles in popular periodicals romanticize the Shakers' handcrafts and indicate no awareness of their technology. Experts do not dispel this view, often noting the inventions of the Shakers but minimizing or overlooking their commitment to technology. Sprigg (1975, p. 28), for example, states: 'Shakers did mechanize some of their handwork if the machines proved more efficient, but on the whole they realized that no machine could put as much care or perfection into any article as an individual could! Andrews (1932) does not mention the mechanization of the sisters' industries, emphasizing instead the hand looms and the spinning wheels of the early decades. In a later work (1963, p. 230), when he describes the end of the century, he says only: 'Knitting machines were introduced, and new industries inaugurated, such as the manufacture of cloaks, coonskin gloves, carpet whips, shirts, and rugs'.

drudgery as their natural burden; instead, they used, maintained, and even invented labor-saving devices to improve their commercial enterprises and to relieve their domestic chores. The zest with which Shaker women seized upon new technology is apparent in one sister's description of a steam-powered engine newly installed in their small commercial sewing industry: 'The engine works *more* than satisfactorily, *it works most charmingly!* . . . attended to by one of the sisters . . .' (*Manifesto*, 1885; p. 168).

The Shakers' devotion to technology grew out of their deepest religious convictions. As two Shaker eldresses explain, the Shaker 'sees no virtue nor economy in hard labor when consecrated brain can work out an easier method . . . and thus the world is richer for many tangible proofs of the Shaker's consecrated ingenuity' (White and Taylor, 1904; p. 310). Industrious, the Shaker's did not over-work; they sought balanced lives of labor, recreation, and spiritual refreshment. Such was the concept of their founder, Ann Lee, once an illiterate textile worker and cutter of hatter's fur in the grim factories of eighteenth-century Manchester, England. From her experience of oppressive toil, she envisioned another, more rewarding life. 'Hands to work and hearts to God', she urged her followers. Work, yes, but there was more to life than a numbing drudgery.

Accordingly, the Shakers' commitment to labor-saving machinery for women's occupations had additional religious roots, in the egalitarian views inherent in their beliefs. Founded by one woman and led during their greatest expansion by another, Lucy Wright, the Shakers believed in a dual masculine–feminine deity. Rather than a trinity that they regarded as all-male, they worshipped a quaternity: Father–Holy Mother Wisdom–Son (Jesus)–Daughter (Ann Lee). Under the Shaker system of eldresses and elders, deaconesses and deacons, and trustees and ministers of both sexes, equal leadership was expected from men and women. Women, obviously, were not the natural servants of men.

In contrast to the outside world, where for much of the nineteenth century married women had no rights to possessions or wages, in Shaker societies women and men lived and produced communally. The assignment of traditional domestic tasks to Shaker women should not obscure the significant fact that Shaker sisters also produced articles for commerce—shirts, bonnets, capes, canned goods, herbs, medicines, to name a few. Shaker women were valued not only as domestic workers but as breadwinners in their communities, where all shared and owned alike.

To Shaker thinking, then, ingenious inventions could as easily be the products of women's minds as men's. The official Shaker periodical lists the accomplishments of non-Shaker women inventors (*The Shaker Manifesto*, 1882, p. 142; *Manifesto*, 1890, p. 164), and pays homage in its pages to the Shaker inventor Sarah Babbitt. Known as Sister Tabitha, Babbitt created her inventions in 1810 in the Shaker society at Harvard, Massachusetts. Years later, a Boston newspaper's interview with Sister Tabitha's cousin, Eldress Eliza Babbitt, then 93 years old, describes the inventor's methods:

'To her genius is due the introduction of the cut nail. She got the idea from watching the operation of making wrought nails. She conceived the idea of cutting them from a sheet of iron when it should be rolled into the desired thickness. Her idea was put into practical operation and found to be a success, and the wrought nail became a thing of the past.

One day while watching the men sawing wood, she noted that one half the motion was lost and she conceived the idea of the circular saw. She made a tin disk, and notching it around the edge, slipped it on the spindle of her spinning wheel, tried it on a piece of a shingle and found that her idea was a practical one, and from this crude beginning came the circular saw of today. Sister Tabitha's first saw was made in sections and fastened to a board. A Lebanon Shaker later conceived the idea of making the saw out of a single piece of metal' (*Boston Sunday Globe*, 1893).

The Shakers also took pride in the invention of another Shaker woman, whose device was intended, characteristically, to lessen drudgery rather than to increase productivity. The two Shaker eldresses report:

'An invention which has greatly lightened the labors of the sisters who do the family baking is in use at Canterbury. It is a revolving oven, the inner body of the oven having four compartments, each presenting its own door. This led to the contrivance of Eldress Emeline Hart, now of the Ministry of New Hampshire' (White and Taylor, 1904; pp. 313–314).

Other inventions that both relieved housekeeping burdens and improved Shaker women's commercial enterprises were devised by Shaker men or by Shakers now unknown. Inventors' names often went unrecorded because Shaker opposition to capitalism caused them to reject patents. As the Shaker eldresses explain, 'To the Shaker, patent money savors of monopoly, the opposite of the Golden Rule. Whatever he invents is for the use of the whole world' (White and Taylor, 1904; p. 310). The eldresses note that Shaker men invented an apple-corer, a washing-machine, a silk-reeling machine, and 'a summer covering for a flat-iron stove, by which the hotter the irons, the cooler the room' (p. 313). Unknown Shakers devised a pea-sheller, a butter-worker, a self-acting cheese-press, the clothes-pin, and three developments in their sewing industries, the latter described by other Shaker sisters:

'The first bird's-eye linen was a Shaker product. Until 1809 when a machine was invented, the cloth was cut with shears made by Shaker blacksmiths. . . . Some of the first irridescent silk was woven in Kentucky, also the Sabbathday Lake (Maine) Shakers made some of the first wrinkle-proof material. This was obtained by placing the cloth between layers of chemically treated paper, pressed in a Shaker invented screw-press, using the heat underneath, producing a shiny surface on one side, a dull water silk on the reverse' (Lindsay and Phelps, 1968).

So keen was Shaker interest in technology that visiting Shakers consistently reported to their home communities the latest developments in sister societies. In 1869, when leaders of the two Kentucky Shaker communities visited the East, one of the eldresses recorded in a diary her fascination with new machinery. At the Watervliet, New York (a society), the eldress notes with enthusiasm:

'Their wash house is well fitted up, the machinery and boiling and all the business being operated by steam, the steam being conducted in pipes to boil the clothes, and heat water etc. A centrifugal clothes dryer instead of a press, which is run by steam. A great improvement. They are then raised to the drying room by windles. This is decidedly the best arranged wash house that I have ever seen' (Smith, 1869).

At the Mount Lebanon, New York (Society's dairy), the Kentucky eldress observed 'a cheese vat, which they report to be a good labour saving arrangement'. The Mount Lebanon herb room also excited her admiration:

We had visited the herb shop in the morning . . . this we found to be an extensive establishment conducted on scientific principles. The machinery is driven by an oscillating (*sic*) engine, the exhaust steam being used for drying herbs, warming the house and heating water, etc. They use coal for fuel, and have a patent drying kiln for drying herbs, and a hydraulic press for pressing them. Altogether it is a valuable Institution' (Smith, 1869).

One of the large dwelling houses at Mount Lebanon, that of the second order, impressed the visiting eldress with its water system. Water from the mountain supplied every story—four in the back and five in the front—and moreover, the water was heated and ran 'both hot and cold', obviously an improvement over the arrangements in Kentucky.

The Enfield (New Hampshire) Shakers, she reports, 'have the best beef chipper I have ever seen, two plain bits set in a wheel turned by a crank', and at their medicinal root shop, 'The machine is driven by water power. It is most complete, simple and effectual'. At Canterbury, New Hampshire, she notes that the Shakers 'have a self presser for the cheese, which they invented here I think they say'. Canterbury also had an impressive washing system:

'In their wash house they have a steam engine to boil the clothes with steam, run their Parker wash mill, which they recommend, and to turn their centrifugal dryer which they also recommend. They have large watertight boxes with two or more apartments, for rubbing and rinsing tubs' (Smith, 1869).

And so it went through the Eastern societies, the Kentucky eldress observing new technology carefully and reporting it with lively interest.

Outside observers, as well, were impressed with Shaker domestic technology. In 1888, a woman visitor wrote an account of Mount Lebanon for a Poughkeepsie, New York, newspaper:

'All the (domestic) work is done by the Sisters who have their seasons of leisure and repose. Running water brought from large springs gushing from the mountain side grinds the grain, churns the butter, rocks the washing machine, cools the huge refrigerator, and being heated, warms the house in winter' (Pool, 1888).

Noteworthy, too, was the Shaker system of sharing work assignments in dining-room, bake-room, and kitchen. The visitor adds: 'Here every step tells, every movement counts. Co-operative work can point to no greater triumph than in Shaker house-keeping'.

A vivid first-hand account of co-operative work and Shaker domestic technology appears in an 1877 report from Canterbury, New Hampshire. Written by 'E. M. H.'—Emeline Hart, inventor of the revolving oven and later the community's eldress—the account describes a winter wash-day:

'The big bell on the house-top began to call us to duty at five o'clock a.m., . . . The weather was intensely cold. . . . Twenty baskets of goods stood waiting the cleansing operation of a Shaker Washing Machine; while as many as twelve sisters were employed for seven hours, at least, as assistants. But what is the matter? The engineer (probably Hart herself) is running too and fro, anon to the loft above, with a pail of hot water, where are two tanks, each capable of holding twelve barrels of water, usually heated by steam and conducted through pipes to the laundry below; but King Frost has breathed his icy breath into the main pipe and congealed just enough of the crystal fluid to obstruct the passage of steam.

   All business is suspended for an hour, at least; yet, believe me, we did not scold or fret; on the contrary, we planned how to fill the time more profitably, and each sister went to perform some little household duty. . . .

After our prudent engineer had administered hot applications sufficient to start the circulation so that hot steam pressed into the water-tanks above, and boiling-tubs below, a dense fog arose, another petty annoyance. . . . We had learned by previous experience, that a current of air from two opposite points would speedily remove the greater part of such a vapor, so we searched for the doors, intending to open one of the east and the other on the west side of the room; but every aperture was as hermetically sealed with ice as a can of fruit ought to be from air. . . . After several fruitless attempts, and a hearty laugh at our defeat by fog, we tried the effect of a good fire. . . .

But the end is not yet; our washing machine next appeared to be frost-bound and out of joint, merely because we had made everything else right, and there was room for another trouble! A few drops of oil and a little hammering soon coaxed this into good-humor. The "Shaker Washing Machine" has rendered us too much valuable service in the last ten years to permit us to underestimate its many excellences. . . . For an hour every pulley and shaft seemed to operate like magic; but suddenly the wringer in the north-west corner (a very cold place) was seized with the epidemic and refused to move; the application of oil, even, nor of much kind treatment could effect a cure. The main-belt had been newly but improperly laced; the same was relaced, and we succeeded in starting the wringer! But . . . we were obliged to pause many times, for nothing would succeed, except a thorough repairing of the belt in question. Finally, good luck attended us, and by one o'clock p.m., our washing was completed. The garments had been mill-washed, boiled, rinsed, wrung and hung to dry, not by one poor Bridget, however, but by a dozen pairs of willing hands dictated by cheerful hearts' (Hart, 1877; p. 36).

The latter aspect of the experience—the cheerful attitude of the workers at their shared task—was important to the author, who notes that her purposes in writing were 'to act as an artist in sketching several scenes . . . secondly, to note the spirit of kindness which prevailed during the performance of this duty'. Hart cites an additional advantage of the Shaker way: 'I have somewhere read that cold and badly-cooked dinners are another annoyance on this ill-fated (wash) day; we, on the contrary, found a warm dinner awaiting us, and kind sisters who prepared the same, manifestly pleased to enhance our comfort in some way'.

Not only their domestic machinery but their commercial technology as well were highly valued by Shaker women. Toiling long hours at their machines, these women emphasized that their working methods were superior to those in the outside world. They often wrote poems decrying the lot of the factory woman, and they insisted that theirs was a far preferable life. Indeed, they had much greater variety, for they rotated their work assignments, moving to another duty every few weeks. A Mount Lebanon sister comments in 1892: 'The Sisters made white shirts, by water power. The younger sisters are the operators; they run the machines eight hours a day and frequently change employments' (Anderson, 1892; p. 101). As other Mount Lebanon women insisted, their occupation was an improvement over the factory work it resembled:

'We have been busily engaged since last April in the making of shirts, but not like the poor factory girls, in their pent up rooms, deprived of pure, fresh air and the healthful sunlight, but in our beautiful, well-ventilated room, that is lighted by seven or eight large windows. Here we cheerfully work, striving to do all we can for the interest of our home. . . . We have made 11,172 shirts, and during the last four weeks we have made 1,920. If you could see our machines run, you would not be surprised at my statement (*Manifesto*, 1889, p. 274).

Women of the smaller Shaker society at Enfield, New Hampshire, also pointed out the pleasant surroundings in which they worked:

'The Sisters are busy, as usual, making custom shirts for Hewins & Hollis of Boston. They have their work rooms in the fourth story of the large Stone Dwelling. From this height they have a very picturesque view of the surrounding scenery. The garments are made mostly by hand-sewing, although they have several Wheeler & Wilson machines which may be used as occassion requires. The Sisters average about six dozen shirts per month. Another company are employed in the manufacture of "Sweaters", (a heavy knit shirt), and of late have been quite busy' (*Manifesto*, 1890; p. 19).

In other societies as well, the sisters used and maintained machinery. From Hancock, Massachusetts, Sister Fidella Estabrook reports: 'In the Church family we use the "Davis Swing Churn", and those who manage it consider the churn a success' (Estabrook, 1894; p. 167). The churn was water-powered by means of an aqueduct in the dairy. As early as 1842, a power loom was introduced at Canterbury, New Hampshire (Frost, 196–) and a visitor there a half century later wrote that she saw a similar loom and knitting machines, fuelled by a wood-burning engine. Another engine supplied power to churn butter, wash clothing, and pump water. Clearly awed, the visitor adds: 'There were forty pounds of steam in the boiler, though Jennie, the Shaker girl who runs it said, "that is rather more than is really needed"' (*Boston Transcript*, 1892).

Canterbury women also took pride in their type-setting machine, introduced in 1882. The sisters became compositors for the Shaker periodical, an occupation they clearly enjoyed. Five years later, when the Canterbury sisters acquired a press, they took over the printing of all Shaker publications (*Manifesto*, 1895; pp. 14–15).

Not only did Shaker women value their technology, but they also understood the mechanical principles involved. In 1885, when Watervliet, New York, sisters obtained a new steam engine, they were obviously delighted. It was, one writes with pleasure, a

'No. 2 "Shipman Engine" rated at full one horse power, to drive from 7 to 8 Sewing machines; the power is ample, and, no doubt is sufficient to drive still more machines if desired.

The engine works *more* than satisfactorily, it works most *charmingly!* requiring no engineer; is attended by one of the sisters, a few moments, about four times a day, simply to supply the oil, and see that the water is duly supplied, without interruption by the engine's pump. . . . Said engine is a wonderful *David* of a *Giant*' (*Manifesto*, 1885; p. 168).

As knowledgeable as she was enthusiastic, the sister concluded with a long technical description of the engine's many merits. The fire-box, she notes, was surrounded by water, so that no heat is wasted by radiation'. And the engine was safe, boasting a newly invented diaphragm that put out the fire if the steam rose beyond the required pressure. 'Besides this, for double guard, there is a safety, or pop valve', she adds appreciatively. The engine could raise a head of steam in 10 minutes, or even in 5, and it appealed to Shaker thrift by running 10 hours on '5 gallons of Kerosene Oil, at a cost of $32\frac{1}{2}$ cts'.

Although technology could be exhilarating, there were occasional drawbacks: power was not always available. At Canterbury, New Hampshire, the sisters were troubled by a water shortage in February, 1895: 'As all our Laundry work and our machinery for knitting and for printing are dependent upon steam power, we are forced to shut down and wait . . . for the snows to melt' (*Manifesto*, 1895; p. 66). In the fall of that year, the Mount Lebanon women report: 'For a short period we had to use a steam motor for shirt work, but upon the 12th the long looked for rain refreshed the earth and enabled us again to use water power' (*Manifesto*, 1895; p. 280). Despite seasonal problems, however, the Shakers regarded their machinery as truly the products of 'consecrated brains'.

The Shaker attitude toward technology was shaped by the optimism and naiveté at the heart of their Utopian spirit. Toward the end of the century, aging and dwindling in numbers, the Shakers continued to look forward to a better world in which technology would play its part. The elderly members of the South Family at Enfield, Connecticut, must have speculated about this future, for a sister, Maria Witham, notes that 'we believe electricity will make us independent of ice in a few years; it is in the air, that creamers and cooling-rooms, will be refrigerated by machinery' (Witham, 1895; p. 43). On another level of speculation, Eldress Catharine Allen of Mount Lebanon, in an essay called 'Democracy', lists goals she proposed for the nation. Characteristically, her first point advocates 'Universal and equal rights of suffrage without regard for sex, race, or creed', and a later point focuses on technology: 'Inventors should be liberally rewarded by the government, and the benefit of new inventions left free for all, as the present system often gives opportunity for large and unjust monopolies, and frequently leaves the real inventors unrequited'. These steps were necessary, Eldress Catharine maintains, 'to achieve true democracy' (Allen, 1895; pp. 200–201).

Linked to their innocent optimism for America's future, the Shaker concept of technology implied a means of realizing their humane social principles, outgrowths of their most profound religious convictions. The machine, they believed, meant life without drudgery. Ironically, the technology the Shakers so admired helped doom them. Industrialization would attract their youth to the teeming cities, and with its shoddy mass-production, force Shaker industries to extinction.

REFERENCES

Allen, Catharine. 1895. Democracy. *The Manifesto* September, pp. 200–201.
Anderson, Martha J. 1892. Health notes among the Shakers, No. 2. *The Manifesto* May, p. 101.
Andrews, Edward D. 1932. *The Community Industries of the Shakers*. Univ. of State of New York, Albany.
Andrews, Edward D. 1963. *The People Called Shakers*. Dover, New York.
Boston Sunday Globe. 1893. Rpt. in *The Manifesto* 1899, February, pp. 23–25.
Boston Transcript. 1892. Rpt. in *The Manifesto* 1892, July, p. 250.
Estabrook, Fidella. 1894. *The Manifesto* July, p. 167.
Frost, Marguerite. 196–. Canterbury Shakers, Canterbury, NH. N.d., n.p.
Hart, Emeline. 1877. *The Shaker* May, p. 36.
Lindsay, Bertha and Phelps, Lillian. 1968. *Industries and Inventions of the Shakers*. Canterbury Shakers, Canterbury, NH. N.d., n.p.
The Manifesto. 1885. July, p. 168. Ibid. 1889. December, p. 274. Ibid. 1890. January, p. 19; July, p. 164. Ibid. 1892. May, p. 101. Ibid. 1895. January, pp. 14–15; March, p. 66; December, p. 280.
Merton, Thomas. 1966. Introduction. In: Andrews, Edward Dening and Andrews, Faith eds. *Religion in Wood: A Book of Shaker Furniture*, Indiana Univ. Press, Bloomington, Indiana.
Pool, Hester A. 1888. Among the Shakers. *Poughkeepsie Eagle*. Rpt. In: *The Manifesto* November, pp. 252–253.
The Shaker Manifesto. 1882. June, p. 142.
Smith, Betsy. 1869. Unpublished manuscript. Diary of a journey by the Ministry of South Union and Pleasant Hill (Kentucky). *Shaker Collection, Library of Congress*. Container 1, Reels 2–3.
Sprigg, June. 1975. *By Shaker Hands*. Knopf, New York.
White, Anna and Taylor, Leila S. 1904. *Shakerism: Its Meaning and Message*. Rpt. 1971. AMS Press, New York.
Witham, Maria. 1895. *The Manifesto* February, p. 43.

Women's Studies Int. Quart., Vol. 4, No. 3, pp. 321–340, 1981.
Printed in Great Britain.

0148–0685/81/030321–20$02.00/0
Pergamon Press Ltd.

WOMEN AND MICROELECTRONICS:
THE CASE OF WORD PROCESSORS

Erik Arnold

Science Policy Research Unit, The University of Sussex, Falmer, Brighton, U.K.

Lynda Birke

Biology Department, The Open University, Milton Keynes, Bucks, U.K.

and

Wendy Faulkner

History and Social Studies of Science, The University of Sussex, Falmer, Brighton, U.K.

Synopsis—The use of microelectronics in production has serious implications for working people, but these implications differ between women and men.

We look first at long-wave (Kondratiev) and classical (Marxist) economic theory relate the effects of microelectronics to the economic system. But this tells us nothing about whether the impact of microelectronics differs between the sexes, because the relevant economic categories are sex-blind. The impact on women can only be analysed by introducing the idea of patriarchy. Thus, the interests of capitalists as an oppressor-class and men as an oppressor-sex can be seen as interwoven but not necessarily always coincident.

Socialism and feminism oppose different oppressive dynamics, yet a victory for one without a victory for the other would be incomplete. Word processing is an area where socialist and feminist struggles can be joined in a practice which is truly progressive.

INTRODUCTION

It is generally agreed that the development of microelectronics has profound implications for people's lives, both in terms of work and of leisure. The implications have, however, only been sketchily explored. The aim of this paper is to discuss ways in which the new microelectronic technology is likely to affect women, and it focuses on office work because this is an area of predominantly female employment upon which microelectronics is likely to have a significant effect, both in terms of job loss and in terms of the nature of the jobs which remain.

In this paper we consider two specific questions. First, we consider briefly what are the general effects of technological innovations upon labour. This is an area which has been the basis of recent debate within the Marxist literature (see, for example, Braverman, 1974; Cooley, 1976).

We consider it here in order to provide a framework for the central question: what are the specific effects of technological change on *women's* employment? As many feminists have recognized, one effect of microtechnology is likely to be considerable job loss, which will particularly affect women in secretarial and clerical work; a second important effect is likely to be on the division of labour and consequent social relations within the office. Here we are particularly concerned with changes in patriarchal relations as a consequence of the introduction of microtechnology. We have focused on office work as a sphere likely to be affected by microtechnology, although the new technology clearly has profound implications for women's employment in other spheres, including in the manufacture of microelectronic components themselves.

'Patriarchy' is frequently defined in rather vague terms, often implying an ahistorical psychic phenomenon with little material base. As a result, interpretations of the concept vary enormously, as several feminists have pointed out.[1] In the era of monopoly capital, patriarchy takes on a different form from, say, in feudal society.[2] These variations make the development of a feminist theory of patriarchy an urgent task, as Beechey (1979) notes. Such a theory has to account for both the independence of patriarchal relations from the means of production, as well as for the connections between them. Nonetheless, some generalizations are possible, and for our purposes in this paper, we will use Hartmann's (1979) definition of patriarchy as 'a set of social relations between men, which have a material base, and which, though hierarchical, establish or create interdependence and solidarity among men that enable them to dominate women.'[3] We choose this definition because it emphasizes that patriarchy is not solely social relations between women and men.

Microelectronics is a generic term for the development of transistor technology which 'integrates' numbers of electronic components into a single 'chip' of semiconductor material—normally, very pure silicon. The earliest versions of these integrated circuits were produced in 1960, and contained the equivalent of only a few discrete components. By contrast, at the time of writing, sample chips containing a quarter of a million components are available. Initially, integrated circuits were developed mainly for military applications where their small size commanded a premium price, but later the civilian market became more important as mass-production brought the costs per item down. The term 'microelectronics' came into use as large scale integration of circuitry was achieved. It encompasses all 'chip' applications, including computer memories and microprocessors,[4] as well as goods aimed at the domestic market, such as plug-in TV games.

We can think of most tasks in terms of 'thinking' and 'doing' components. As Braverman (1974) and others have pointed out, the introduction of new technology has forced a greater and greater split between these components, as well as providing management with greater control over all aspects of the process of production. Electronics has made it possible, in many cases, to automate the 'thinking' component where this component can be reduced to a set of rules or instructions. The significance of microelectronics lies in the fact that it is much less expensive to process information in this way, thus making it economic to displace labour further. Since office work is concerned primarily with processing information, and has so far been little affected by automation (compared to manufacturing processes),[5] the potential effect of automation via microelectronics is very large—larger, indeed, than in manufacturing

---

[1] For example, see McDonough, R. and Harrison, R. 1978. Patriarchy and relations of production. In: Kuhn, A. and Wolpe, A.-M. eds. *Feminism and Materialism: Women and Modes of Production*. Also, see Hartmann, H. 1979. The unhappy marriage of marxism and feminism: towards a more progressive union. *Capital and Class*.

[2] Indeed, some writers use the term 'patriarchy' to refer to that form of male dominance which characterized the feudal family, rather than using it as a term generalizable to other historical epochs. See Ehrenreich, B. and English, D. 1978. *For Her Own Good: 150 Years of the Experts' Advice to Women*, p. 11.

[3] This is the definition applied by Hartmann, *op. cit.* p. 11. She also points out that 'the material base on which patriarchy rests lies most fundamentally in men's control over women's labour power. Men maintain this power by excluding women from access to some essential productive resources (in capitalist societies, for example, jobs that pay living wages) and by restricting women's sexuality'. We would distinguish here between 'patriarchy' and 'sexism'. A social system might be patriarchal, that is, it is organized in such a way that men systematically oppress women and gain material advantages through that oppression. 'Sexism' is what happens at the level of interpersonal relations, when individuals act out that oppression.

[4] A microprocessor is a small computer which uses microelectronics either made from a small number of integrated circuits, or recently, in the form of a 'computer on a chip'.

[5] The productivity of U.K. manual workers was increased through automation by some 83 per cent between 1960 and 1970, compared with 4 per cent for office workers. At present, capital invested per office worker is about 10 per cent of that per shopfloor worker. See Stewart, Tom. July 1979. How to design a workable system. *Word Processing Now*, Business Systems and Equipment/Maclean-Hunter Ltd., London.

since the latter is already highly automated. The majority of those employed in processing information in offices are currently female (98.8 % of typists and secretaries are women), and it is clear that women will be the principal losers in office automation.

Although we are specifically concerned in this paper with women's work, we intend to discuss more general consequences of technological innovation first, to provide a base from which to argue points about the changing nature of women's secretarial work. In doing so, we draw on material which clearly does not offer a feminist analysis, although it provides a necessary framework from which to consider the impact of the new technology on one field of women's work. Finally, since many of the technical terms employed here are likely to be unfamiliar to some readers, we have included a glossary.

1. ECONOMICS, TECHNICAL CHANGE AND MICROELECTRONICS: INEVITABLE UNEMPLOYMENT?

Change in industrial processes and products which increases labour productivity (the amount produced per person) is far from being a new phenomenon. In industrial capitalism, the effect is frequently to displace labour: to put people out of work. One famous example of this type of technical change is the introduction of power looms, which displaced about 210,000 hand weavers between the 1810s and 1850 (Hobsbawm, 1969), while the English output of textiles rose nearly eightfold.[6] Of course, technical change can save things other than labour: ways might be found to economize on raw materials, or to maintain or increase output with fewer or cheaper machines, and so on. Neoclassical economists such as Samuelson (1965) have pointed out that capitalist firms are interested in *any* technical innovation, provided that it reduces their total costs. On the other hand, innovation can be used to secure supernormal profits; as the changes spread, competition between capitalists brings prices down and profits return to normal levels (Schumpeter, 1961). Thus, a general result of technical change in manufacturing industry can be reduced prices.

However, theoretical approaches which treat production as simply a matter of combining anonymous 'factors of production' assume away differences in the nature of these factors. In particular, the neoclassical approach ignores the fact that labour (like management) is human and *behaves*. Workers may participate in strikes and combinations, or find ways of exercising control over their labour. As we discuss later in this article, for instance, women in an office control their working conditions in many ways. Because of these tendencies, management is likely to be especially interested in labour-saving technical change: replacing labour with machines has several advantages, as has long been recognized:

'The great feature of our modern mechanical improvement has been the introduction of self-acting tools. All that a mechanic has to do is, not to labour, but to watch the beautiful functions of the machine. All that class of men who depended on mere dexterity, are set aside altogether. . . . By these mechanical contrivances I reduced the number of men in my employ, 1500 hands, by fully one half. The result was that my profits were much increased.' (Nasmyth, 1851, on the invention of the steam-hammer in response to the engineers' strike. Quoted by Rosenberg, 1976.)

---

[6] Calculated from Deane, Phyllis and Cole, W. A. 1962. *British Economic Growth 1688–1959: Trends and Structure*, p. 213. It is interesting to note the form that the weaver's own demands took in protesting against the power loom: they protested against '. . . the adaptation of machines, in every improvements, to *children* and *youth*, and *women*, to the exclusion of those who ought to labour—THE MEN'. Cited from a Yorkshire weavers' report by Thompson, E. P. 1968. *The Making of the English Working Class*, p. 335.

Cooley sums up the advantages of employing machines in production:

'In the human/machine interaction, the human being is the dialectical opposite of the machine in that he is slow, inconsistent, unreliable but highly creative, whereas the machine is fast, consistent and reliable, but totally non-creative' (Cooley, 1980).

Not only is machinery less recalcitrant than labour, of course: it also becomes part of the property of the capitalist, as Marx recognized in his distinction between "living" labour (i.e. human workers) and "dead" (i.e. past labour embodied in the means of production).

The neoclassical economists are, of course, right to insist that entrepreneurs economize on any available factor of production. The strength of the older, classical tradition (to which Marx himself belongs) is that it recognizes that labour has attributes which make it difficult to manage. It may become economical to change the technique of production so that costs, including labour costs, are minimized: but over and above its price relative to other factors, living labour uniquely has qualities which make it managerially desirable to replace it.

Most of the technical changes with which we are familiar occur within only one sector of industry: the steam-hammer was invented to replace manual hammering; the commercial production of aircraft may or may not affect employment in other transport industries, and so on. These *intrasectoral* technical changes have tended to lower prices, and to cause only frictional unemployment (if any) as people displaced from one sector find work in another. Economic growth makes this process easier. Freeman has pointed out that labour-displacing technical change may not necessarily have significant effects on employment and economic growth:

'A process of labour-displacing technical change at the level of the firm is not in principal inconsistent with steady growth and relatively full employment at the macro-level, provided certain conditions are satisfied, including mobility and adaptability of labour, and a level of new investment sufficient to absorb the displaced labour plus any growth of the labour force' (Freeman, 1977; pp. 7–8).

On the other hand, there appear to be no sufficient reasons why labour-displacing technical change and full employment should not, in practice, turn out to be inconsistent. This would be the case if a technical change occurred not at the level of the firm or sector, but at the macro-level: the level of the economy.

Economists have identified a number of fairly short economic cycles, such as the 'Kitchin' cycle, lasting about 40 months, and the 'Juglar' cycle of about 10 years. Relatively little attention has been given, however, to the much longer waves lasting about half a century, the so-called 'Kondratiev' waves. Kondratiev originally published 'The Long Waves in Economic Life' in German in 1926, arguing that the Western World had to date experienced two and a half long waves beginning more or less with the Industrial Revolution.

'First long wave:
  (1) The rise lasted from the end of the 1780s or beginning of the 1790s until 1810–1817.
  (2) The decline lasted from 1810–1817 until 1844–1851.
Second long wave:
  (1) The rise lasted from 1844–1851 until 1870–1875.
  (2) The decline lasted from 1870–1875 until 1890–1896.
Third long wave:
  (1) The rise lasted from 1890–1896 until 1914–1920.
  (2) The decline probably begins in the years 1914–1920.'
(Kondratiev, 1935; p. 111).

These waves, then, are associated with periods of growth and consolidation, followed by economic recessions, such as the depression of the 1930s and the 'Hungry Forties', and the Great Depression (1873–1896), the Great Slump (1929–1933) and—potentially—a new depression in the 1980s.

There is not agreement about what causes the Kondratiev waves, but a number of attempts have been made to link social phenomena with it. Kondratiev himself (1935) discussed the relationship with changes in techniques, wars and revolutions, the assimilation of new countries into the world economy, and fluctuations in gold production, while Schuman and Rosenau (1974) discuss other social changes, including the rise of feminism, in relation to the Kondratiev wave.

The suggestion has been made by Freeman (1978a), however, that the Kondratiev waves are associated with important new technologies: the first with steam; the second with the railways; the third with automobiles and electrical and chemical engineering; and the fourth—in which we appear to be beyond the point of inflection where upswing turns into downswing—with electronics. Initially, the new technologies bring vast increases in employment—several million jobs—and rising wages, partly because of skill shortages:

> 'After about a quarter of a century, the new technologies and branches of industry are now firmly established, and their role as generators of additional new employment dwindles. Whereas in the early boom days, price competition among the firms involved in the new activities was not severe and new firms were attracted by the prospect of high and profitable growth rates, now competitive pressures within the industry become stronger. While capital intensity grows, labour-saving and material-saving technical change are increasingly important' (Freeman, 1978a; p. 20).

This pattern matches at the macro-level that discerned for individual industries.[7]

If Freeman is correct in making this association, then one way of classifying technical changes might be by their *pervasiveness*: some technical changes pervade the entire economy and thus influence the Kondratiev cycle, while others only influence one or two industrial sectors. The frictional technological unemployment which may accompany the latter is mainly associated with problems of adjustment and mobility; while the former may result in major structural unemployment. Our experience of electronics since the Second World War fits in well with this pattern. The automation scare of the 1950s and 1960s proved to be unfounded, and electronics—notably in the form of computers—became all-pervading. Rather, employment grew for a while, notably in the electronics industry (an industry which employed considerable numbers of women in production).

Microelectronics may be seen, then, as the maturing, consolidating, technological component of the electronics Kondratiev wave. Its importance lies not in the novelty of the processing which it can perform, but in the quantum reduction it brings in the cost of manipulating information. Hence, many tasks which it was previously thought uneconomical to automate can profitably be automated by means of microelectronics—a fact which has considerable implications for labour:

---

[7] For cycle theories of industrial innovation, see Abernathy, William J. and Townsend, Philip L. 1975. Technology, productivity and process change. *Technological Forecasting and Social Change*, pp. 379–396. Also Mueller, Dennis C. and Tilton, John E. 1969. Research and development costs as a barrier to entry. *Can. J. Economics* **2** (4), 570–579.

'(Microelectronics) . . . makes it possible to improve the quality and increase the speed of production, but its most important economic function is that the processes by which man adapts nature to his needs, and, in particular, the production of material goods can be made more and more automatic, and so require less labour time from men and women themselves . . . it is clear that new scientific knowledge and new techniques must result in considerable social and political instabilities, since they are radically changing the central core of the economic system, the basic processes and relations of production' (Bodington, 1973; pp. 85–86).

In other words, as the processes of production become increasingly automated, fewer and fewer people will be required in production.

There are two important unknowns about the pervasiveness of microelectronics. First, we do not yet know *how* pervasive it will be, how important economic and social barriers to the diffusion of microelectronics will be. Second, we do not know what happens when commodities are produced using little or no labour. How can a small number of highly productive people operating an automated process, together with the capitalists who employ them consume as much as they produce? And how do the displaced workers acquire the means to consume?

If there is decline in manufacturing employment, then either large-scale unemployment follows, or the slack is taken up elsewhere in the economy. One prevalent idea is that this slack is taken up largely in service industries[8] (Bell, 1974). This idea is, however, highly questionable, since there is evidence that despite increasing real wealth, the expenditure of U.K. consumers on services has actually declined between 1954 and 1974 (Gershuny, 1978). What has increased is expenditure on consumer durables which actually replace service expenditure: television instead of cinema; washing machines instead of laundries, and so on. More significantly, this decline has considerable implications for women, since women's employment in the past has been somewhat protected by the expansion of the service sector. This limited protection, however, is likely to disappear as jobs in the service sector— including office work—become rationalized with the development of microelectronics (Breugel, 1979).

It seems, in fact, that rather than service industries taking up the slack, the increased tertiary employment is associated with a changing balance between occupation categories, related to the production of goods. Most people are now employed in jobs related to the increasing control of management over production: jobs such as advertising, quality control, work study, personnel management, design, research and development (Braverman, 1974)— mostly, in fact, office jobs. Yet a contemporary office is barely more productive than its predecessor a century ago, when it comes to handling text: arguably, the main increase in productivity has come by means of the photocopying machine. Set alongside continual increases in productivity in manufacturing processes, this might explain the shifting balance of employment from shop floor to office-based jobs. But automation is likely to drastically increase office productivity, and could well be a factor in reversing the trend towards a high ratio of service to production jobs within manufacturing industry. The implications of this for women's employment are not good.

It would seem, then, unlikely that the slack will be taken up elsewhere. As the need for

---

[8] Although it is worth noting that microelectronics applications include the capital equipment used in service industries, so that we might expect some labour displacement here too.

labour in offices declines, there is not likely to be a corresponding increase in labour requirements in manufacturing itself. In the U.K., both the State and the Trades Union Congress have made substantial commitments to furthering microelectronic technology—which puts the trade unions in the invidious position of supporting a technical change which is already putting large numbers of people out of work. It is, of course, now impossible to opt out of microelectronics, even if we thought it desirable. Both the cheapness of microelectronic components and their reliability militate against the use of earlier technologies because the firm which does not use microelectronics is at a competitive disadvantage. Thus, at the level of decision-making in firms, it is necessary to balance the loss of *some* jobs through the use of this new technology, against the loss of all jobs in the firm as a result of competitive failure. Given the capitalist relations obtaining in international trade, the same logic holds at the level of the nation state: use the technology and lose some jobs, or face the consequences of becoming internationally uncompetitive.[9]

Thus far, we have pointed out the inevitable introduction of microelectronics, and have noted that we are now entering a period of economic recession associated with the new technology. Both the recession and the impact of the technology on production generally are likely to cause massive unemployment. However, as Braverman has pointed out, the impact of new technology on labour is more than effects on job loss alone: new technology tends also to influence both social relations and the division of labour (Braverman, 1974; pp. 184–235).

2. DETAIL DIVISION OF LABOUR

In discussing the division of labour, a distinction can be made between social and detail division of labour: 'in spite of the numerous analogies and links connecting them, division of labour in the interior of a society, and that in the interior of a workshop, differ not only in degree but also in kind' (Marx, 1970; p. 354). While the social division of labour divides people in such a way that they each produce commodities (tradeable goods), the 'detail labourer produces no such commodities. It is only the common product of all the detail labourers that makes a commodity.... Division of labour within the workshop implies the undisputed authority of the capitalist over men, that are but parts of the mechanism which belong to him' (Marx, 1970; pp. 355–356).

Increasing the detail division of labour has certain advantages for capital, as Babbage,[10] writing in 1835, recognized:

> 'That the master manufacturer, by dividing the work to be executed into different processes, each one requiring different degrees of skill or force, can purchase exactly that precise quantity of both which is necessary for each process; whereas, if the whole work were executed by one workman, that person must possess sufficient skill to perform the most difficult, and sufficient strength to execute the most laborious, of the operations into which the work is divided' (Babbage, 1835; pp. 175–176).

---

[9] This logic, therefore, applies also to the public sector, with the reservation that there is some scope for a political decision not to use a labour displacing technical change. This scope is, however, limited by the strength of the productive base and the amount of economic 'efficiency' in the public sector which that base can support.

[10] Charles Babbage is best known for his work on calculating machines or mechanical computers, for use in the preparation of mathematical tables and similar tasks. Often regarded as 'the father of the computer', his attempts to process information mechanically in the mid-nineteenth century were defeated by the impossibility of obtaining metal parts machined to a sufficient degree of accuracy.

This is what Braverman calls the 'Babbage principle': dividing labour cheapens some or all of the detail operations involved because the appropriate 'grade' of labour can be applied to each detail task:

'The capitalist mode of production systematically destroys all-round skills where they exist, and brings into being skills and occupations that correspond to its needs. Technical capacities are henceforth distributed on a strict "need to know" basis. The generalized distribution of knowledge of the productive process among all its participants becomes, from this point on, not merely "unnecessary", but a positive hindrance to the functioning of the capitalist mode of production' (Braverman, 1974; p. 82).

Thus, workers under capitalism perform increasingly specialized but simple tasks. They become increasingly dependent on the capitalist because they lose the skills required to make commodities under a social division of labour. Increasingly, too, they lose touch with the workings of their tools—as far as the word processor operator in the office is concerned, it is simply not relevant to understand how the machine works.

F. W. Taylor—the crusader for 'scientific management' or 'Taylorism'—was a crucial figure in articulating management's need to maximize its control over the work process. Braverman has identified three principles in Taylor's ideas. First, management must control knowledge about the productive process. This involves both the detail division of labour to which we have referred, and the knowledge embodied in the machinery used; both result in deskilling. Second, conception and execution must be separated in the work process. Conception becomes the exclusive prerogative of management. Third, the resulting monopoly of knowledge must be used to control every step of the labour process and its mode of execution (Braverman, 1974; pp. 112–119). If we now consider the effects of introducing word-processors—microelectronics—into the office, we can see how it will essentially increase management's control over the work process along the lines of Taylor's three principles.

3. WORD PROCESSING IN PRACTICE

In offices, we see labour being divided in different ways according to the size of the office. In larger offices, the function of secretary is split into personal assistant and typist. Other specialized functions appear, such as card punching, photocopying, switchboard, filing and post-room work, and these become associated with their own, specialized technologies. The introduction of word processors is likely to integrate and change many of these specialized functions. Together with this increasing detail division of labour comes increasing control by management of the work process: that is, control over work which is largely done by women.

(a) *Management control*

In line with Taylor's three principles, word processing, first, deskills the job of typing; second, it removes most of the decisions remaining in the hands of the typist in the pre-existing division of conception and execution between author and typist; and third, it increases the extent to which the typist is tied to her desk ('workstation') and reduces the extent to which she is free to pace her own work. A crucial factor is the skill characteristics of the pool of labour available to management. Even typing itself involves varied tasks at present: changing paper, typing, arithmetic for text centring, page layout and so on. Word processors deskill the typing tasks by means of such facilities as easy correction, automatic text centring and automatic layout. Thus, while still requiring some basic ability to operate a standard keyboard, word processors dispense with the need for layout skills and high levels of keystroke accuracy.

From the management point of view, methods are more precisely specified and their use more readily monitored. While secretarial work at a typewriter involves opportunities to regulate the work by taking a trip to the stationery cupboard, having chats with the other office staff, waiting for the correction fluid to dry and so on, the word processor removes these elements of regulation and enforces management's perception of the operators' proper function: pressing keys as fast as possible. As Barker and Downing (1980) point out, bosses have traditionally turned a blind eye to these ways of pacing work by typists and secretaries. This is, however, likely to change as word processing enables greater control to be exerted over text production. Additionally, the machine normally incorporates the ability to monitor the typist's rate of work by recording the number of key depressions. This means that management's control over the work process increases dramatically, and becomes more naked. It makes it virtually impossible for typists to 'cover' for each other, or to slip away for a few moments. In short, it can mean the end of what Braverman calls the 'social office' (Braverman, 1974; p. 344) as far as ordinary typists are concerned, and industrializes their work. Like the imposition of the factory system on the spinners and weavers of the late eighteenth century, it 'brings the tyranny of the clock, the pace-setting machine and the complex and carefully timed interaction of processes' (Hobsbawm, 1969; p. 85).

The fact that word processors are used under management control makes a crucial difference to the process of using them. Because they eliminate retyping and simplify the process of changing the text, word processors are potentially liberating for people doing work for themselves: they save time and effort. But time-saving is not necessarily liberating for people who are *employed* to operate word processors. Under these circumstances, the only freedom the machine gives to the operator is the freedom to go on the next job: the capitalist appropriates the time and effort saved by the machine.

(b) *Centralized control?*

Centralized (generally shared-logic) word processing systems offer the technology for automating the typing pool and hence displacing labour. Because it raises labour productivity in this way, word processing offers an additional economic rationale for centralized typing. Word processing tends to be currently thought of as essentially a centralized activity, and analyses tend to be based on this assumption. However, in 1978, only about 8 per cent of the workstations sold in the U.K. were part of shared-logic systems (Cox, 1978). The proportion of shared-logic systems sold is generally expected to rise, but 'stand-alones' (i.e. single station word processing units) will remain numerically more important for some time, and are expected to account for 60–70 per cent by 1983 (Wharton, 1978).

There are some technical reasons why the prevalent idea of word processing as an essentially centrally-organized activity may be inadequate. The parallel with computing is important: computers have until recently tended to be 'mainframes'—huge, central machines onto which many functions were hung in order to use expensive common elements (e.g. central processor and memory) as intensively as possible. The declining cost and improved performance of electronic components has led to the phenomenon of 'distributed processing'; that is, using several mini-computers spread throughout the firm instead of a mainframe to handle information more conveniently. These mini-computers can often be run inefficiently, such as by asking them to do less than they are capable of, or by running them for only limited periods each day. This contrasts with the intensive 24-hr operation of expensive mainframes. The crucial factor in this change has been the fantastic decline in the cost of computing power, both in terms of money and space.

As the demand for word processing increases, it is likely that the cost will decline dramatically, making a stand-alone barely more expensive than an electric typewriter.[11] This fall in cost may increase the proportion of word processing that is not centrally organized, although word processors may increasingly be able to communicate with each other and with computers. It would also eliminate the need claimed by some organizations to run a twilight shift in order to obtain maximum use from the equipment. This tendency towards single unit, rather than centralized, word processing has implications for the social relations which operate between women and men in the office. These will be discussed in the next section.

4. THE INTRODUCTION OF WORD PROCESSORS AND WOMEN'S WORK

As we pointed out earlier, definitions of patriarchy tend to be vague. Interpretations vary widely, even among feminists. For this reason, many have turned to Marxism as a body of theory which arguably explains the power relations associated with the capitalist mode of production as an analytical framework within which to consider power relations between the sexes. However, as Hartmann (1979, pp. 7–8) points out, the very analytic power of Marxism has tended to obscure its limitations with respect to sexism: 'Marxist categories, like capital itself, are sex-blind'. For example, although Marxist analyses might explain why and how particular people fill particular places, they give no clues about why *women* are subordinate to *men* inside and outside the family and why it is not the other way round (Hartmann, 1979; p. 8). More specifically, such analysis cannot readily provide us with a clear forecast of how the introduction of word processing will affect women's work in offices, simply because Marxism has traditionally paid scant attention to the specific role of women in capitalist society. We have, so far, used the Marxist framework to look at the logic of technological innovation within capitalistic relations of production: we will now look specifically at patriarchal relations.

We foresee three major ways in which the introduction of word processing will affect women's work in offices. First, it will influence the class basis of secretarial work; second, it will lead to some job loss for women, with possible consequences for opportunities open to women; and third, it will have considerable implications for the nature of patriarchal social relations within the office. We will deal with each of these in turn.

(a) *Class basis*

One important effect of word processors is the discontinuity in skill (and other) requirements between the 'typist/word processor' operator and the 'secretary/personal assistant' levels. It seems likely that this gap will widen as word processors are introduced into offices. Braverman (1974) has described how the introduction of new technologies tend to downgrade the lower status, routine jobs, and to curtail any opportunities for advancement. He cites two illustrative examples from data processing:

---

[11] The typewriter's electromechanical parts are already at a stage of development where neither their raw material nor their production costs offer further significant cost reduction: the technology is 'mature'. The same is not yet true of word processor components, notably the electronics and the software.

'At one bank, "Due to the simplicity of operator training for single pocket proof encoders (a keyboard operating task), the job, as related to our job evaluation scale, has been downgraded three grades and reduced from an average base of $68 to $53 per week".... Elsewhere, the job of coder is characterized thus by a data-processing executive: "The only gal who will stick with this work has to have a husband with two broken legs and five hungry kids. No one else could stand it"' (Braverman, 1974; p. 337).

He also cites the American Management Association:

'To be honest—we don't want people to take data processing jobs as stepping-stones to other jobs. We want permanent employees capable of doing good work and satisfied to stay and do it. To promise rapid advancement is to falsify the facts. The only rapid advancement for the bulk of non-supervisory data-processing staff is *out of data-processing*' (Braverman, 1974; p, 338).

Of course, it would be misleading to imply that there are no class differences already in secretarial work; in general working-class women are unlikely to enter the super-secretary/personal assistant category, and are more likely to end up in the typing pool.

'For working-class girls to be accepted into this type of world they have to learn to develop middle-class ways of operating within their femininity; a "natural" telephone voice, a perfect dress sense, perfect grooming, etc. What this means, is fitting "submissively" into the gentlemanly professional atmosphere of serious business—displaying the correct attitude of deference to the big decision-makers—playing the whiter than white Madonna. The other side of the couplet—the whore—is more befitting the inhabitants of the typing pool where the girls can "have a laugh" when (usually only when) men aren't around' (Barker and Downing, 1980; p. 77).

Working class women are also likely to have had different educational opportunities and to have, as a consequence, more limited aspirations.[12] This division will worsen as resources are increasingly withdrawn from the public sector into the private sector (thus further limiting the education provided for the majority of children), and as the distinction between 'secretary' and 'typist' becomes more pronounced. Opportunities to 'advance' from the typing pool towards personal assistant status were always severely limited for women of working-class background, at least partly because of the educational opportunities open to them. If automation further separates the 'thinking' from 'doing' components of information processing, then those chances of promotion disappear altogether.

Another effect of technological innovation in production is to 'proletarianize' other groups of workers. As Cooley (1980) points out, many people in white collar jobs—including, for example, scientists and technologists—are now facing redundancy, where once this danger only faced those in manual trades. The introduction of word processing may similarly affect the jobs of those in lower management—indeed, there are indications that this is already occurring (Barker and Downing, 1980). While women very rarely make their way into top level management, some have succeeded in entering lower management. With even these jobs at risk as a result of microelectronics, yet another avenue is closing for women.

---

[12] A number of authors have pointed out that the present educational system is an inherently unequal one, which serves to reproduce the social division of labour required by capital. See, for example, Bowles, S. 1976. Unequal education and the reproduction of the social division of labour. In: Dale, R., Esland, G. and Macdonald, M. eds. *Schooling and Capitalism: A Sociological Reader.*

(b) *Unemployment risks and women's place*

There is little doubt that considerable unemployment will follow the introduction of microelectronics; an estimated 20 per cent of the workforce is expected to lose their jobs in the postal service, for example, by the end of the decade (Wintour, 1980). As we have already indicated, this may in part be due to the downswing of the economy associated with the 'electronics Kondratiev' wave; and in part it will be aggravated by an increase in the rate of growth of the available labour force in the early 1980s (Freeman, 1978b). This increase in unemployment will, of course, be felt in all sectors, but we are here concerned with the effects on women's employment opportunities. Job opportunities for women are likely to deteriorate, both as a consequence of labour-displacing effects of automation, and of the tendency of employers to view female labour as more easily displaceable (Barron and Norris, 1976). There is a contradiction here, however. As Anthias (1980) has pointed out; '... in *practice* women can be both a cheap *and* disposable labour force' (emphases in original). The capitalist, unlike capital, is not necessarily sex-blind. For the employer, women workers have a number of important and useful characteristics which distinguish them from male workers; they have low levels of skill and training; they are poorly trade unionized; they exhibit a high turnover, particularly among young office workers; and, as Marx noted, the employment of women helps to break down male workers' resistance to capitalist development (Beechey, 1978).

It is sometimes argued that women form a large part of Marx's 'reserve army of labour', which can be called upon if needed, and just as easily made redundant. However, as Anthias argues, this category does not 'of necessity' include women, and it ignores some of the essential features of female employment in capitalist society.

> 'Most importantly, it marginalizes the importance of women's employment for advanced capitalism—their role as cheap labour and as a relatively unorganized and passive element in the workforce. It also marginalizes the importance of the occupational categories and industries that women are active within, an importance that has yet to be fully delineated' (Anthias, 1980; p. 61).

Clearly, women have and will be called upon to join the work-force at times when there is a shortage of labour. But their role within the 'reserve army' will depend, in the end, on the type and level of skills required at any one time. An overall reduction in the number of workers required in offices will cut off a major (and up until recently) growing avenue of female employment. In the absence of more positive educational and employment policies, job opportunities for women will decline.

It is, of course, impossible to predict or evaluate the extent of actual job loss; unemployment statistics as they are usually collected tend to understate both the number of people out of work, and to give a distorted picture of exactly *who* is out of work at any one time. Probably the biggest distortion is that official statistics ignore large numbers of women. There are two reasons for this; first, much female employment is casual or on the fringes of industry (outwork for example; West, 1978); and second, women tend to be ignored as a consequence of the prevailing ideology which maintains that women's primary social role is within the family. As West notes:

> 'Numerous assumptions and practices—the social security and taxation systems, trade union policies, and so on—reinforce the notion that women are, or should be, economically dependent on men, and among these is, of course, the reproduction of the deskilled, low-wage sector itself' (West, 1978; p. 249).

There are many ways in which this ideology is manifest in British family policy, and these have been explored in detail elsewhere (Land, 1976). It is pertinent to note, however, that two significant aspects of the emphasis on the dependent wife are that (a) women have less entitlement to unemployment benefits (McIntosh, 1978), and (b) only those women registering at the labour exchange in Britain are counted as unemployed, so that official statistics severely underrepresent the true number of women seeking jobs (Breugel, 1979).

Although we are unable to predict the extent of the unemployment, it seems likely that female unemployment will increase. What might be the consequences of this important change for the social role of women?

One obvious inference which might be drawn from the likelihood of major female job loss is that 'there will be increased subtle persuasion that our place is in the home' (Collins, 1979). This is a point often made in feminist writing, commonly with reference to the pro-natalist ideology of the 1950s. It was undoubtedly true that the 1940s and 1950s were a period of ideological onslaught, in which the family was seen as central to women's lives (see, for example, Birmingham Feminist History Group, 1979): but does it necessarily follow that an increase in women's unemployment will result in such an onslaught now?

We should distinguish here between the removal of facilities which enable women to seek wage labour—nurseries, crèches, and so on—and a period of increased *ideological* onslaught in the form of propaganda persuading women that their rightful place is in the home. The two might well coincide, but not necessarily so. Both bear a complex, and ill explored, relationship to the needs of capital.[13] Welfare provisions, such as crèches, are not something given to women by a beneficent state, as McIntosh (1978) points out.

We are already seeing a concerted reduction in the provision of welfare services of this sort, as a result of the changing needs of capital. Advances made in nursery provision in the later 1960s and early 1970s are now being lost to enormous cuts in public expenditure. And it is undeniable that the loss of such provisions worsens the employment prospects for women.

'Ideological onslaught' is another matter though. Pro-family ideology operates at all levels of the capitalist state, and has existed at least since the beginning of the 'family' as we now know it. However, this ideology becomes at times more transparent or direct, and we are subjected to a barrage of books and articles reminding us of the importance of the home, and the joys of motherhood. It might be supposed that these periods of increased propaganda coincide with periods of economic recession and consequent unemployment, but this is not necessarily so. The pro-motherhood ideology of the later 1940s and 1950s, for example, occurred at a time of unprecedented economic growth.[14]

If we are are to look at the role such ideological onslaughts have for capital, then we should look more closely at the periods in which the ideology is most evident, and at whom it appears to be directed. Ehrenreich and English (1978) have analysed some of the ways in which such ideology is levelled at women, and note that different standards are set for women

---

[13] As McIntosh (1978) pointed out, although the historical materials are there, a detailed analysis of the relationship of welfare provision to the needs of capital still has not been done. See McIntosh, 1978. pp. 280–281.

[14] In saying this, we distinguish between ideology serving different functions. The pro-natalist ideology referred to here seems to be aimed at persuading middle-class women that their rightful place is at home. In times of rising unemployment, however, there is likely to be an increase in ideology which differentiates between different sectors of the workforce. Such notions are not aimed at those affected, but serve to persuade employers, that for some 'innate' reason, certain workers are better than others, e.g. whites rather than blacks, men rather than women and so on. We suggest that any reference to ideological onslaught should consider the function served for capital by the *form* that the ideology takes.

from different class backgrounds; they describe, for example, the massive propaganda around the turn of the century eulogizing women's work in the home, and creating a science and management of domestic work. The values inherent in this propaganda were middle-class, although the ideologues of the new domesticity tried to extend them to the working-class, often by way of charity workers.

These periods of increased ideological onslaught seem to coincide primarily with periods of economic growth, rather than recession—periods such as the turn of the century, or the more familiar 1950s. The removal of facilities such as nurseries, on the other hand, may be more characteristic of periods of recession. But either way, women are the losers.[15] Suggesting this is not, of course, to deny that many women will be *forced* to remain at home, rather than persuaded by pro-natalist ideology: with rising unemployment, and the destruction of childcare provisions, this seems almost inevitable. Other social changes might follow too. For example, in the slump of the 1930s, large numbers of women and men faced unemployment, and those few women lucky enough to retain a job found themselves under considerable pressure, as Rowbotham notes:

' "Rationalization", wage cuts, the substitution of women for men, sped up, and the reduction in the power of the trade unions through unemployment meant that there were objective reasons for antagonism between men and women workers. There was a widespread belief that the employment of women had actually caused unemployment' (Rowbotham, 1974; p. 129).

The trade unions remained ambiguous in their treatment of women, and so did little to help.

Trade unions have been traditionally male-dominated, at least in part because the activity of women in the trade union movement was for a long time channelled off into 'separate development' (Davies, 1974). As a result, the unions have tended to share the view of patriarchal capitalism that is is men's employment which is fundamental, and women's, marginal. In 1877, for example, Congress was arguing that: 'the duty of men and husbands is to bring about a condition of things when their wives should be in the proper sphere of home instead of being dragged into competition of livelihood with the great and strong men of the world' (Davies, 1974; p. 63). Although unions are less blatant today, there are numerous instances of trade unionists acting specifically against women (Counter Information Services pamphlet, undated). And, of course, what is argued at Congress about equal pay and women's rights is not necessarily carried out in practice: the activity of the TU movement around equal pay legislation has aptly been described as 'apathetic' (Snell, 1979). Some of the unions are aware of the potential problems which could follow the introduction of the new technology, but to what extent they address the specific problems which women face remains to be seen.

(c) *Social relations within the office*

As Braverman has pointed out, the introduction of new technology tends to transform the relationship between capital and labour: more and more control over the process of

---

[15] This does not, of course, distinguish between women of different classes. A lack of nurseries is more likely to hit working-class women, while, as Ehrenreich and English (1978) point out, the pro-family ideology to which we refer is aimed primarily at middle-class women.

production is removed from the hands of labour to the hands of management. This process serves to create a:

'"labour force" in place of self-directed labor; that is to say, a working population conforming to the needs of this social organization of labor, in which knowledge of the machine becomes a specialized and segregated trait, while among the mass of the working population there grows only ignorance, incapacity, and thus a fitness for machine servitude. In this way, the remarkable development of machinery becomes for most of the working population, the source not of freedom but of enslavement, not of mastery, but of helplessness, and not of the broadening of the horizon of labor, but of the confinement of the worker within a blind round of servile duties in which the machine appears as the embodiment of science and the worker as little or nothing' (Braverman, 1974; p. 194–195).

These transformations are likely to follow the introduction of microelectronics into offices. But, in addition, the technology has implications for the specifically patriarchal nature of social relations within the office, simply because nearly all the workers likely to be affected are women.

In office work, women workers have to fulfil a unique function: that of 'office wife'. Secretarial staff are generally expected to be attractive and 'ladylike', as well as efficient. In fact, their status rarely derives directly from the expertise they have to offer a firm, but rather from that of the man (or men) for whom they work. As Barker and Downing note:

'The status of a secretary within a particular organization is dependent not so much on her level of "skill" and ability to work to a high degree of efficiency using her own initiative, but on the status of her boss and concomitantly on her ability to manipulate modes of femininity which are specifically middle class. . . . Status is *the* decisive factor in the (office) hierarchy' (Barker and Downing, 1980; pp. 76–77, emphasis in original).

The role of the 'office wife' is determined by patriarchal social relations in that her role is subordinate to, and services, the men in the firm (or the particular man for whom she works), just as wives service men in the home. In the classic instance, the office organization chart will show a division of labour within a predominantly male group. Tacked onto this division is the scattered group of (overwhelmingly) female secretaries. Thus, while the 'bosses' work directly towards organizational goals, the secretaries only do so indirectly, by acting as servants to the 'bosses'. It is our contention that the hierarchy implicit in these patriarchal relations will be intensified by the advent of the new technology.

As we pointed out earlier, the introduction of mechanization serves to enhance management's control over the labour process. In this respect, the introduction of word processing technology will serve a similar purpose. But it must also be said that it enhances *male* control over *female* labour. Barker and Downing have noted that deskilling takes on an added significance when applied to female office work:

'. . . conventional notions of skill and deskilling cannot be applied to a predominantly female labour process because the very fact of a job being labelled "women's work" brings in enormous ideological determinations which enable its skill content to be "somehow" devalued. Apart from high speeds in shorthand and typing, secretarial workers require special qualities which can only be learnt through an apprenticeship in womanhood and in this sense the notion of "deskilling" takes on a different tone' (Barker and Downing, 1980; p. 93).

In this situation, the bulk of the skills required of a word processor operator will be increasingly male defined. Sexist though the interpersonal relations in an office undoubtedly are at present, a secretary/typist has at least some control over how she apportions her time and her tasks. In this sense, a part of the job is 'hers' and is directly under her control, thereby giving a limited degree of independence. Barker and Downing comment on the existing office culture:

> 'The significance of the culture we have attempted to describe is that it is indeed a factor in the reproduction of women's oppression, but it can also be seen as the development of an informal work culture which cannot be penetrated by "masculine" work standards. In other words, it constitutes a world in which the male bosses (and their underlings) cannot penetrate, thus allowing the women to get away with doing certain things which cannot be controlled' (Barker and Downing, 1980; p. 83).

With the introduction of word processors, however, this situation changes.

We noted earlier that current trends in word processing technology are toward stand-alone units, rather than centralized units. It is sometimes argued, or implied, that the word processor operator is effectively removed from the opportunity for sexist interactions, since she is operating at a workstation with little or no direct contact with the originators of the work. However, the effect on sexist interactions is likely to be less dramatic in most cases if stand-alones are used. An organization may utilise several small stand-alone units, with each operator 'working for' a small number of individuals (usually men). These will thus perpetuate the boss/secretary type of contact. The opportunity for sexist interactions may be slightly reduced, since the operator is more tied to her workstation than a typist is to her typewriter, but the patriarchal nature of her relationship to those individuals for whom she works remains. It hardly seems justified to conclude, as Barker and Downing do, that:

> 'Word processors are an attempt to achieve this (reduction in the time lost through personal interactions) by the *replacement* of patriarchal forms of control by more direct capitalist forms of control' (Barker and Downing, 1980; p. 85, our emphasis).

Patriarchy is not likely to disappear from offices simply because word processing reduces the number of occasions on which sexist interactions can take place between women and men.

Although the overall number of secretarial staff will be reduced by the introduction of word processors, we foresee a situation in which most of those who remain as word processor operators will still be involved in personalized boss/secretary types of relationship. Whilst the situation is similar, the woman's small degree of independence and control over the pace of her work are gone: her boss now has considerably more control over the quantity and quality of her work,[16] and she has little opportunity to move about the office, to talk to other people, and so on. Furthermore, as her productivity is increased, there is a greater possibility that she will have to work for several 'bosses', all of whom can perpetuate sexist interactions. It seems likely, then, that the patriarchal hierarchy, in which women are subordinate to men, is only likely to be reinforced and intensified by the advent of word processing technology. More than ever, the typist of the new era will be the office wife and Braverman's 'social office' will disappear.

---

[16] The person to whom she is immediately responsible may not be the person who assumes ultimate control over the production process, of course. However, his control over the secretary's work is still direct, and is likely to be increased as her productivity increases.

CONCLUSIONS AND SUMMARY

In this paper, we have explored some of the possible implications of microelectronics for women. Word processing provided a convenient focus for this, and one which has important similarities with the rest of the information sector. Technically, word processing and other types of information processing are converging (Barron and Ray, 1978). This is illustrated by a number of current developments, such as the ability of word processors to communicate with each other, and with computers; the incorporation of limited calculating ability into word processors; and the text-editing capability of mini-computers. These developments mean that most clerical, information-handling jobs may in future be done on the same, or similar, equipment. Word processing will then serve as a paradigm case for clerical jobs— which are at present chiefly held by women.

This electronic future is likely to unfold in the context of economic recession—possibly the downswing of a Kondratiev wave. The consequences, both in terms of rising unemployment and the intensification of prevailing social relations, are bleak. They appear, however, to be a logical result of the conjunction of capitalist and patriarchal relations in our society.

These conclusions may seem gloomy. However, we feel that there are few grounds for optimism at the present time. Indeed, the situation for women in clerical and secretarial work could become worse than we have described as technology is developed for analysing speech and translating it into machine code—thus dispensing altogether with the typist. What is gloomy is the introduction of these new technologies into the existing social order. We might think of alternative, more socialist, modes of production centred on the new technologies, and using them for human benefit. But these are unlikely to obtain in the majority of offices given present social relations. Nevertheless, we can try to offset some of the adverse effects expected as a result of the new technology, as at least some of the trade unions have recognized.

From the point of view of the trade unions, however, two points must be made. First, since, under capitalism, machines embody capitalist relations of production, a responsive, defensive posture is likely only to amount to a foot-dragging exercise, an opportunity for propaganda and consciousness-raising. But this can only be a short-term tactic, because if new technology is not accepted, together with the loss of *some* jobs, competition might eliminate the employer, or induce the firm to relocate. Management is well aware of this as a means of persuading recalcitrant employees to accept new technology: this was the point on which the problems between unions and management hinged during the recent year-long strike by employees of *The Times*. Second, it must be understood that it is only through seizing control of technology that production processes can be devised which do not necessarily embody capitalist relations of production, and which are capable of producing socially useful commodities. There have been some attempts to mobilize rank and file workers within specific industries to this end—for example, the establishment of the Lucas Aerospace Corporate Plan, which has greatly reduced the impact of management plans for redundancies and closures.

However, a trade union position which deals with capitalist technical changes on a *purely* class basis ignores the problems which beset *women* within patriarchal capitalism. In this sense, class activity can be as sex-blind as the Marxist analytical categories which describe it. Patriarchy and capitalism involve particular forms of social organization which, as has been argued elsewhere, go hand-in-hand (Hartmann, 1979). It is no answer to turn away, as some members of the Left have done, from women's issues as trivial, unimportant compared to the fundamental issues of class solidarity in the face of rising employment. Hartmann comments:

'The pressures on radical women to abandon this silly stuff (i.e. feminism) and become serious revolutionaries have increased. Our work seems like a waste of time compared to "inflation" and "unemployment". It is symptomatic of male dominance that our employment was never considered to be a crisis. . . . A struggle aimed only at capitalist relations of oppression will fail, since their underlying supports in patriarchal relations of oppression will be overlooked' (Hartmann, 1979; p. 24).

One hopeful outcome, however, might be that the increasing pressure on women's job opportunities encourages their further unionization. It is only when more women become *active* members of the trade unions that there is any hope of changing the unions' attitudes towards women's right to work, and hence any hope of their fighting to defend women's jobs. The danger at the moment is that the impending recession forces the labour movement into defensive strategies, in which feminism is all too easily omitted. Our strategy must be to ensure that feminism is on every agenda, including that of the trade unions. Word processing and its associated technology can provide an important arena in which union and feminist struggles can be joined in practice.

Acknowledgements—We are grateful to Hilary Rose and to Sue Himmelweit for helpful comments on the earlier draft of this paper, as well as to anonymous referees. Several members of the Science Policy Research Unit at the University of Sussex discussed ideas with E. A. while this paper was being written.
We would also like to thank John Krige and Ed Sciberras for detailed comments on earlier drafts.

GLOSSARY

Classical economics. Economics (roughly) from Adam Smith to Alfred Marshall (including Marx): regarded value as related to the expenditure of *labour* in production: interested in the division of labour and technical change at the level of the individual plant or firm.

Factor(s) of production: Factor(s). Inputs to a productive process such as raw materials, labour, capital: economic analysis of technical change is often conducted as if there were only two factors: capital and labour.

Frictional unemployment. Unemployment which is caused not by a lack of *enough* jobs but by a lack of jobs of the right kind: commonly, frictional unemployment results when the jobs available are not in the same areas as the potential workers or need different skills to the ones possessed by the available unemployed workers: frictional unemployment can be overcome by relocation, retraining, etc.

Microelectronics. The development of semiconductor (transistor) technology which 'integrates' large numbers of semiconductor components onto wafers of silicon via a combination of photographic reduction, etching and layer deposition techniques under conditions of strict cleanliness: also known as 'integrated circuits' (ICs) or 'chips'.

Microprocessor. A microelectronic component which contains logic circuitry for 'processing', e.g. calculating: when combined with electronic memory and input–output circuitry it becomes a computer: recently this has been done on one 'chip' of silicon, producing a 'computer on a chip'.

Neoclassical economics. Economics (roughly from Alfred Marshall to date: the tradition taught in schools and universities (principal text-books are by Samuelson, Lipsey and Leftwich): regards value and price as equivalent: generally assumes that technical change can be analysed adequately at the level of the economy rather than of the firm, and does this analysis in terms of the different 'rewards' paid to factors of production before and after the change.

Stand-alone word processor. Word processor which has one keyboard and operates independently of other machines by having its own processor (usually a microprocessor), memory and printer: it is self-contained.

Shared-logic word processor. Word processor which shares one processor (the 'logic') and memory between two or more keyboards, so that two or more people can operate it simultaneously: has one or more shared printers.

Structural unemployment. Unemployment which is built into the structure of industry, insofar as the industrial system needs fewer workers than want work: relocation or retraining do not help, because there are no jobs to relocate or train for.

Word processor. Computerized typewriter: consists of keyboard, processor, memory and printer: may also have a visual display unit (VDU), which looks like a television screen, to display text which is being worked on: can often be connected to a computer, to other word processors, to an optical character recognition (OCR) machine (which 'reads' material that has been typed using a special typeface, normally on a golfball typewriter) or phototypesetting machine.

Workstation. The console, keyboard and visual display unit (if present) where electronic information processing work is done by the operator—in this case, a word processor.

REFERENCES

Abernathy, William J. and Townsend, Phillip L. 1975. Technology, productivity and process change. *Technological Forecasting and Social Change* **7** (4), 379–396.

Anthias, F. 1980. Women and the reserve army of labour: a critique of Veronica Beechey. *Capital and Class* **10**, 50–63.

Babbage, Charles. 1835. *On the Economy of Machinery and Manufacturers*, 4th edn. Charles Knight, London.

Barker, Diana Leonard and Allen, Sheila eds. 1976. *Dependence and Exploitation in Work and Marriage*. Longmans, London.

Barker, Jane and Downing, Hazel. 1980. Word processing and the transformation of patriarchal relations. *Capital and Class* **10**, 64–99.

Barron, Iann and Curnow, Ray. 1978. *The Future of Information Technology*. Report to CSERB, Department of Industry, Science Policy Research Unit, (mimeo), Brighton.

Barron, R. D. and Norris, G. M. 1976. Sexual divisions and the dual labour market. In: Barker, Diana Leonard and Allen, Sheila eds. 1976. *Dependence and Exploitation in Work and Marriage*. Longmans, London.

Beechey, Veronica. 1978. Critical analysis of some sociological theories of women's work. In: Kuhn, Annette and Wolpe, Ann-Marie. 1978. *Feminism and Materialism: Women and Modes of Production*. Routledge and Kegan, Paul, London.

Beechey, Veronica. 1979. On patriarchy. *Feminist Rev.* **3**, 66–82.

Bell, D. 1974. *The Coming of Post-Industrial Society*. Heinemann, London.

Bodington, S. 1973. *Computer and Socialism*. Spokesman Books, London.

Bowles, S. 1976. Unequal education and the reproduction of the social division of labour. In: Dale, R. *et al.* eds. 1976. *Schooling and Capitalism: a Sociological Reader*. Routledge and Kegan, Paul and the Open University Press, London.

Braverman, H. 1974. *Labour and Monopoly Capital: The Degradation of Work in the Twentieth Century*. Monthly Review Press, New York.

Breugel, Irene. 1979. Women as a reserve army of labour: a note on recent British experience. *Feminist Rev.* **3**, 12–23.

Collins, Sue. 1979. Women and chips. *Spare Rib* **83**, 19–22.

Cooley, M. 1976. Contradictions of science and technology in the productive process. In: Rose, H. and Rose, S. eds. 1976. *The Political Economy of Science*. Macmillan, London.

Cooley, M. 1980. *Architect or Bee? The Human Technology Relationship*. Hand and Brain Publications, Slough, U.K.

Counter Information Services. Undated. *Crisis: Women Under Attack*. Anti-Report No. 15. CIS, London.

Cox, A. C. *Word Processing Digest:* cited in industry discussions.

Dale, R., Esland, G. and McDonald, M. eds. 1976. *Schooling and Capitalism: A Sociological Reader*. Routledge and Kegan, Paul and the Open University Press, London.

Davies, Ross. 1974. *Women and Work*. Arrow Books, London.

Ehrenreich, Barbara and English, Deirdre. 1978. *For Her Own Good: 150 Years of the Experts' Advice to Women*. Anchor Press, New York.

Freeman, C. 1977. *The Kondratiev Long Waves: Technical Change and Economic Development*. Holst Memorial Lecture, Science Policy Research Unit, (mimeo), Brighton.

Freeman, C. 1978b. *Government Policies for Industrial Innovation*. J. D. Bernal Lecture, Birkbeck College, London.

Gershuny, Jonathan. 1978. *After Industrial Society? The Emerging Self-Service Economy*. Macmillan, London.

Hartmann, H. 1979. The unhappy marriage of marxism and feminism. *Capital and Class* **8**, 1–33.

Hobsbawm, Eric. 1969. *Industry and Empire*. Pelican Economic History of Britain, Vol. 3. Penguin, Harmondsworth, Middlesex.

Kondratiev, N. D. November 1935. The long waves in economic life. *Rev. Economics Statistics* **17** (6).

Kuhn, Annette and Wolpe, Ann-Marie. 1978. *Feminism and Materialism: Women and Modes of Production*. Routledge and Kegan, Paul, London.

Land, Hilary. 1976. Women: supporters or supported? In: Barker, Diana Leonard and Allen, Sheila eds. 1976. *Dependence and Exploitation in Work and Marriage*. Longmans, London.

Marx, Karl. 1970. *Capital*, Vol. 1, (trans., Samuel Moore and Edward Aveling). Lawrence and Wishart, London.

McDonough, R. and Harrison, R. 1978. Patriarchy and relations of production. In: Kuhn, Annette and Wolpe, Ann-Marie eds. 1978. *Feminism and Materialism: Women and Modes of Production*. Routledge and Kegan, Paul, London.

McIntosh, M. 1978. The state and the oppression of women. In: Kuhn, Annette and Wolpe, Ann-Marie eds. 1978. *Feminism and Materialism: Women and Modes of Production*. Routledge and Kegan, Paul, London.

Mueller, Dennis, C. and Tilton, John E. 1969. Research and development costs as a barrier to entry. *Can. J. Economics* **2** (4), 570–579.

Rosenberg, Nathan. 1976. *Perspectives on Technology*. Cambridge University Press, Cambridge.

Rowbotham, Sheila. 1974. *Hidden From History*. Pluto Press, London.

Samuelson, Paul A. 1965. A theory of induced innovation along Kennedy–Weizsucker lines. *Rev. Economics Statistics* **47** (4), 343–356.

Schuman, J. B. and Rosenau, D. 1974. *The Kondratieff Wave*. Delta, London.

Schumpeter, Joseph A. 1961. *The Theory of Economic Development: An Inquiry into Profits, Capital, Credit, Interest and the Business Cycle*, (trans. Ribers Opie). Oxford University Press, Oxford.

Snell, M. 1979. The Equal Pay and Sex Discrimination Acts: their impact in the workplace. *Feminist Rev.* **1** (1), 37–57.

Thompson, E. P. 1968. *The Making of the English Working Class*. Penguin, Harmondsworth, Middlesex.

West, J. 1978. Women, sex and class. In: Kuhn, Annette and Wolpe, Ann-Marie eds. 1978. *Feminism and Materialism: Women and Modes of Production*. Routledge and Kegan, Paul, London.

Wharton, K. June 6, 1978. Special report: word processing. *The Guardian*.

Wintour, P. June 6, 1980. Burying the bad news. *New Statesman*, pp. 837–838.

Women's Studies Int. Quart., Vol. 4, No. 3, pp. 341–353, 1981.
Printed in Great Britain.

0148–0685/81/030341–13$02.00/0
Pergamon Press Ltd.

THE CULTURE OF ENGINEERING: WOMAN, WORKPLACE AND MACHINE[1]

SALLY L. HACKER

Department of Sociology, Oregon State University, Corvallis, OR 97331, U.S.A.

Synopsis—Questions arising from research on automation and women's work have led me to explore patriarchal elements in the culture of engineering/management. In an élite technological institute, the engineering faculty, compared with the humanities faculty, reported more distance in childhood from experiences and qualities generally gender-linked with females—intimacy, sensuality, one's own body, social complexity. Engineers valued social hierarchy on a continuum giving most prestige to scientific abstraction, least to feminine qualities. Such values were transmitted in the engineering classroom, for example, through professors' jokes, to a new generation of engineering/management. A persistent mind/body dualism was exhibited, subordinating sexuality and the body, and elevating scientific abstraction. The dualism translated into a mechanical view of the person and to continued separation of functions of mind and hand. Further examination of mind/body dualisms may help us to understand how the persistence of this body of ideas in Western technology affects labor processes, and in particular, women, workplace and machine.

INTRODUCTION: MANAGERS AND THE CULTURE OF ENGINEERING

For the past several years I have studied the impact of technological change on women workers in four industries in the United States—insurance, printing and publishing, agribusiness and telecommunications. In agribusiness, automation and runaway shops have reduced employment for women factory operatives, chicana[2] and white; mechanization of farmwork has reduced employment among migrant workers, male and female. Women farmers faced a double threat—the economics of large scale agrotechnology, and politics which favored male over female farmers (Hacker, S., 1977). Over a 3 year period of technological change in the telephone company, women lost 22,000 jobs while 13,000 more jobs were obtained by men. Automation eliminated operator and entry level clerical work while it simplified male craft jobs to the clerical level, drawing women in, only to push them out again in the next round of automation (Hacker, 1979). Office automation in an insurance company slowed the growth rate in some clerical occupations, following patterns noted by Feldberg and Glenn (1980).

In a newspaper firm, 'cold' typesetting (computer, phototypesetting vs hot metal processes) also threatened male craftwork, as that work became clerical in nature and designed for women workers at much less pay (Hacker, 1980). In this case, however, a strong, predominantly white male union retained the de-skilled work for their members (who referred to it as 'junk' work).

---

[1] Partial support for this research came from a Ford Faculty Fellowship, 1973/1974, Drake University, Des Moines, Iowa and a Mellon Post-doctoral Fellowship in Humanities and Engineering, MIT, 1975/1976. Thanks for critical evaluation from Joan Acker, Mimi and Paul Goldman, Roberta Hall, Roz Feldberg, Fred Pfeil, Bart Hacker; for much editorial help from Joan Rothschild; for help in interviews from Barbara and Ronald Dalton.
[2] Women of Mexican/American descent, largely from the Texas migrant stream.

The more sophisticated technical work created by automation provided employment more often for men than for women—in engineering, management, sales, systems analysis and the like. With some variations, the flow of workers through occupations during technological change appeared to proceed from white male to minority male to female, then machines. In the newspaper firm, this process was short-circuited as white male labor gave way only to machines, designed, managed and often maintained by white males with more sophisticated technical skills.

In all instances, women's home responsibilities, lack of employment options, unresponsiveness of unions, opposition of husbands and male co-workers inhibited women workers' ability to protect their interests collectively. Such factors, and the way in which work is organized, heightened female attrition rates, further easing the processes of automation (Hacker, 1979). Most of these findings fit nicely into a Marxist framework. Sex and race effectively divided the working class, inhibiting solidarity and weakening class consciousness and struggle. Women and minorities functioned as a reserve labor army, particulary useful when a company moves rapidly to capture a new market or to change its technological base (Christoffel and Kaufer, 1970; Braverman, 1974). The benefits of technology go to the owners, not to society in general.

Some parts of the story did not fit quite so nicely, however, such as domination and exploitation of women by husbands, male co-workers, and unions, as well as by corporations (Harmann, 1976; Brown, 1979; Sokoloff, 1980). These factors suggested patriarchal elements at work. Observing the ways managers viewed women within the industries studied, I found views that justified exploitation of women, including easier manipulation of their labor during times of technological change. Such attitudes were prevalent especially among those managers with a technical or engineering background. Most of the managers that I interviewed in the telephone company, for example, had a background in electrical engineering. The engineering/managers in industry seemed especially male-centered, and prone to gender the social and physical world. Activities, styles of interaction, jobs, machines, devices, even bodies of knowledge were often characterized as having masculine or feminine properties, appropriate to men or women. These gender-based perceptions were also stratified, or hierarchically ordered. What was womanly had low status; what was manly had high status. Considered dumb and/or sexy, women were viewed with suspicion and distrust, and were more closely controlled than others.

I was particularly struck by the way managers insisted 'ladies' didn't move. Touring a printing plant, where the head of Research and Development showed us the hand bindery, I observed middle-aged women sitting at a table, stuffing material into covers for binding. 'This is the only place we hire girls in this department', our guide told us. When asked why, he said 'This is boring, routine, detail work. Men won't sit still for that kind of work.' He referred to *Ms.* magazine, which the plant printed, as 'the porno department'.

In a poultry plant, I learned that 'people won't take these jobs anymore, but women and migrants will because they expect less.' Management reported that farm women worked out best in deboning, because farm men were accustomed to greater freedom of movement and chose beef rather than poultry work. Telephone company job descriptions for traditionally female work read: 'works close to the desk', 'works under close supervision', 'writes in small spaces'. Men's work at corresponding tasks differed largely by the freedom to move about inside and outside the plant (Northwestern Bell Telephone, 1973).

The tendency to polarize male and female, masculine and feminine extended to bodies of knowledge. In agribusiness, 'manly' fields were beef production compared to poultry; crop production compared to horticulture; salesmanship (which stimulated needs) compared to womanly clerking (which simply supplied what a customer wanted).

Agribusiness training classes portrayed women consumers as ignorant, incapable of shopping without male guidance, dangerous when exercising choice, (e.g., choosing vegetable additives, boycotting beef, protesting extensive use of agribusiness chemicals). Women were considered suitable for routine, detail work and child care, which freed the mind of man for decision-making (Hacker, S., 1977).

These observations suggested a relationship between sex and dominance in the organization of industry, that the managers expressing these views most often shared a technical or engineering background seemed particulary worthy of note. Engineering contains the smallest proportion of females of all major professions and projects a heavily masculine image hostile to women (Rossi, 1965; Ott and Reese, 1975). Women are not easily accepted as colleagues by men in the field. Many engineering magazines are liberally sprinkled with advertisements portraying women draped suggestively over one piece of equipment or another. *The Iowa Engineer*, published at Iowa State University, came complete with a centerfold 'E-Girl of the Month' and a dirty joke page. At scientific/engineering conventions, attractive women in bunny suits staff merchandise booths; a tape measure on a scantily clad model illustrates the benefits of the metric system. A university fair booth promotes agricultural engineering with a leather mini-skirted mannequin, a sign on its rear reading, 'Ag Engineering, for a BROAD education.'

These examples reflect a culture of engineering, highly male-centered. Publications, fairs, conventions not only reinforce this culture, but socialize young engineering/managers as well. An earlier, more powerful, socializing agent is the educational institution which trains these future managers. In order to explore further the development of this culture, I spent a year in participant observation and interviewing at a prestigious institute of technology in the eastern United States where the interests of management and technology were closely linked. I sought to find out how and why in this culture the social and physical world may come to be gendered and how and why gender-linked characteristics come to be elevated or subordinated.

What I found were significant mind/body dualisms, a male-linked mind superior to a female-linked body. In the following second Section I will describe findings of my research at the institute that support this view. The third Section will speculate on the meaning and implications of such dualisms for women, workplace and machine.

AT THE ENGINEERING INSTITUTE

The institute was a major point of origin and transmission of engineering culture, as exhibited in the behavior and attitudes of both engineering students and faculty, and in classroom procedures and general atomosphere. I participated in and observed classrooms, seminars, lectures, social gatherings, and conducted a systematic series of in-depth interviews with engineering faculty and a comparable sample of humanities faculty members.

My first impressions reflected perhaps little more than a stereotype of what was a technological milieu. The buildings were large and austere. The place was quiet. Dominant elements appeared to be mechanical and physical rather than social—sophisticated laboratories seemed to both shape and reflect the nature of social interaction. Compared with other campusses where I had studied or worked, presentation of one's physical and social self seemed less meaningful to students, and I met less affect than elsewhere. Male students encountered difficulty with community or cross-campus parties, where the very mention of their institute 'turned off' women, and they were occasionally referred to as 'turkeys'. Many students identified their bodies with machines.

Snyder (1973) has contrasted metaphors among such students ('I need a tune up', 'retool', 'add gas', 'get the carburetor adjusted' etc.) with organic metaphors (e.g. 'cultivating', 'nurturing young plants') common on a nearby women's campus. Students were encouraged not to develop serious relationships with 'girls'. Relationships with females, other than for immediate, specific sexuality, would distract them from their work and drain their energy (Snyder, 1973); hence the qualified acceptance of women students only as 'one of the guys'.

My in-depth interviews with a random sample of members of the engineering faculty—a procedure which produced an all-male sample—and a comparable sample, then, of men in the humanities faculty ($N = 40$) were designed to follow some of these issues in the culture of engineering. I wondered about gender-assigned tasks and behaviors in childhood, such as intimacy in social relations, early experiences with girls, attitudes toward characteristics considered womanly, and toward nature, and the sexualization of technology itself. I hoped to find links between childhood experiences of élite engineering professors and their current values.

When questioned about intimacy in childhood family and friendship relationships engineering faculty reported little: 'Close, within reason'; 'Never very warm in exchange of feelings'; 'Never dependent on others in an emotional sense . . . could be quite happy on a desert island'; 'I didn't have personal feelings as a child'; 'Most men even now seem to be able to form warm relations . . . but not especially intimate.' Others described theselves as shy, and suggested that 'an interest in learning how things worked' might insulate one from social relations or substitute for them. Humanities faculty recalled a little more intimacy, but stressed the negative as well: 'Close and contemptuous.' More typically, they, also, recalled 'strong barriers to communicating emotional things'.

Relationships with girls were not a source of childhood pleasure for either group. One engineer said, 'They weren't my ball of wax.' Others were 'intimidated by girls'; 'ignored them'; 'felt insecure about them'. Most spoke of all-male play groups, schools and colleges. At one boarding school, boys were punished for talking to girls in town. Some humanities faculty reported a friendship with a girl in childhood, but most were like engineering faculty in being segregated from girls and 'puzzled' or 'mystified' or 'frightened' or 'shy and insecure'.

Questions about sexual experiences tended to yield mere 'yes' or 'no' answers. But another question touching on physical pleasure of a particular kind—'Were you good at, or interested in sports or athletics as a child?'—produced some unexpected responses. The engineering faculty I interviewed were generally attractive and robust in appearance. But two-thirds of them painfully recalled children's bodies that would not do what they should: 'I was fairly uncoordinated'; 'painful experience'; 'never very good at sports'; 'started out rolypoly and pudgy'; 'I was really awful'; 'a sissy'; 'sickly'; 'I wasn't courageous'. One recalled being picked last for the playground team; another, his fear of having the ball hit toward him as he stood alone in left field. Another worried about embarrassing a gung-ho father. Others recalled attempts to compensate for physical shortcomings by 'being head of the class' in everything else. (These results were shared with those interviewed. One pointed out they had likely advanced in school grade more rapidly than their peers, and were therefore 2 or 3 years younger than classmates.) In contrast, among humanities faculty, many also had felt incompetent in sports as a child, but did not seem to care that much. Only one, with a long history of interest in things technical, recalled the strong and painful feelings typical of the engineering faculty.

To explore sensual pleasures, I asked for recollections of pleasures such as the play of sunlight, colored lights, quality and texture of materials, pleasurable tastes and smells, music with good rhythm. About half of the engineers, chiefly those in the more abstract, scientific fields of engineering, recalled no such pleasures. Some thought them abnormal for men, unmanly, or 'my wife's concerns'. (A few recalled visual pleasures of a kite against clouds, reflections from a lake on clear summer evenings, the ripple of sunlight on moving waters; aural play, e.g. with echoes; tactile pleasures sanding wood, walking on snow and the like.) In sharp contrast, almost all the humanities faculty recalled sensual pleasures as a source of much gratification in childhood.

About half of both groups remembered pleasure in being outdoors, in the natural world. Some recalled the pleasures of solitude, 'loved the stillness' of hiking. Most, however, stressed the skills of manipulation of cognitive control, classifying or analyzing, scouting, changing or improving what one found.

I asked these faculty why 'woman' or 'womanly' was associated with nature, why we tend to see nature as female. Avoiding the obvious 'Mother Nature', I quoted Bacon on pursuing nature in her secret paths and similar passages to suggest what I wanted to learn about. No respondent made the association between women and nature himself, but when asked why others might, engineering faculty replied: 'Because of the whole cycle of having periods and all that'; '[to protect women], men are more aggressive'; 'Women end up at home without a direct role in survival . . . childbearing . . . is a little more obviously relevant to nature than to man, nature being growth and reproductive'; 'the earth gives plants as a woman gives children; 'it's a very basic and primitive image'; 'People's interpretation of nature, emotionally, is out of my field . . . the hard side of nature is my business'; 'women and nature look nice'; 'Nature is where everything comes from, including babies.'

For engineering and humanities faculty alike, reproduction is the key linking women with nature in the mind of man. But humanities faculty, unlike engineers, were also apt to comment on aspects of both women and nature seen as unpredictable, uncontrollable and dangerous.

Engineering faculty ranked technical expertise more valuable than knowledge of social relations. They described social sciences in womanly terms: soft, inaccurate, lacking in rigor, unpredictable, amorphous. Very few felt inadequate because they lacked knowledge of social relations or social systems. Almost all, however, felt engineers more qualified than most to move into management. They perceived little difference between managing people and managing technical systems.

At the institute, I found that fields within engineering were also ranked, informally, along an 'earthy–abstract' continuum. Electrical engineering (EE) carried more clout and status than, say, civil engineering. The former was considered 'cleanest, hardest, most scientific'; the latter far too involved in physical, social and political affairs. Most engineers agreed with the stereotype of EE, although those outside that field resented its power and status, merely because the field was closer to abstract science.

In *The Existential Pleasures of Engineering*, Samuel Florman (1976) stresses the sensual and physical, as well as intellectual, pleasures derived from the practice of engineering. However true this might be of others, it was not the picture most EE's painted of themselves.

When asked what it was about their work which gave them most pleasure, their answers suggested something quite different: 'The best hard science is flawless with simple systems [so large] you can deal with them by statistical methods'; 'the mathematical symbology seems to me very pretty . . . can represent so many different things and rather subtle connections'; 'It's very hard to remember enough to put order into nature. You have to have some structure for it always, and that structure is beautiful'; 'reducing to rationality, although it is right on the border, just barely rationalizable'; 'My mother was a hysterical woman ... I think somewhere along the line I felt the need for things you could trust ... That was the attraction of mathematics'; 'Some degree of elegance, aesthetically and technically'; 'The beauty of finding that single equation that sums up everything, that explains everything'.

These are pleasures not unlike those derived from empirical social research. The question is not only why this work is enjoyable, but also why it is so prestigious and highly rewarded. Further, little is to be seen here of the 'crafting' about which Florman waxes so eloquent. That crafting is more likely now left to people without mangerial or decision, making functions, or is incorporated into the machine.

A final question invited comparison of traditional ways of organizing work in industry, along hierarchical lines, with newer non-hierarchal forms: those that rotate tasks and allow workers and professionals to teach each other their skills. (One engineer at this institute had in fact reorganized his laboratory so that engineers, technicians and bottle washers did rotate tasks and shared skills.[3]) Most of the engineering faculty that I interviewed thought such an approach would be wasteful and inefficient. 'Science can only be done by a highly trained élite.' 'The Chinese are lying about what they've discovered [working non-hierarchically] or about how they've done it.' 'It would only give them [lab. workers, secretaries] something to talk about at cocktail parties.' Although a few thought some sharing of tasks, especially crafts, would benefit engineers, no one considered that sharing clerical work would be helpful to them. The humanities faculty contrasted with engineering in that most favored a more egalitarian organization of work. Some of the responses seemed to reflect a common masculine experience among members of both groups. Many men on both engineering and humanities faculties had learned to find pleasure in ordering the natural world. They experienced sex-segregated childhoods and subsequent anxiety about 'girls'. Almost all explained the woman–nature identity in terms of reproductive ability, but humanities faculty added that both women and nature could be dangerous. The engineering faculty tended to differ from those in the humanities in recalling less pleasure of involvement with social or sensual experience, more discomfort with sports or distress about the way a young boy's body should behave. Engineering faculty had also learned to place greater value on hierarchical relations as rational, and on abstract and scientific skills as worthy of greater social rewards than other skills.

In the privacy of an élite institution, where a consensus on some basic values might be assumed, this emphasis on hierarchy was taught to the next generation of engineer/managers in various ways. Classroom humor was an unexpected but clearly effective way to transmit key social values along with technical expertise. In various classes and seminars I auditted (electrical engineering survey, decision analysis, telecommunications, artifical intelligence), professorial humor seemed markedly different from that in the social sciences. In these élite

---

[3] There were other notable exceptions to norms expressed by the randomly selected faculty. One professor in telecommunications devoted his first lecture to a brilliant analysis of social and political ramifications in this field. He noted the increased amount of material to be covered no longer allowed him to integrate this analysis with technical instruction. Others worked uphill against the increasing tendency toward technical rationality. A professor in electrical engineering conveyed the rich language and context of Newton's work on color optics; a chemist analyzed the implications of military research and development on his field; many explored ecologically centered technologies; the director of a technology and values program struggled to salvage it from strong management oriented influences. These were important but definitely variant efforts at the institute (Hacker, 1978).

engineering classrooms, it seemed that wives, students and others with relatively little power were frequently the butt of the joke; there was a fair amount of mildly scatalogical humor as well.

With the help of a graduate student in EE, I conducted a systematic content analysis of jokes in a course on telephone technology taught by two professors and an engineer from the telephone company. This analysis showed students encouraged to laugh at, in order of frequency: (1) technical incompetence; (2) women, and to a lesser extent blacks and workers; (3) honesty or everyday morality; and (4) the body and its functions, through mildly scatological references.

(1) By far the largest proportion (44 per cent) of the 129 jokes recorded in this way focussed on technical competence. Things overly complicated, messy, slow, redundant, cumbersome are the mark of a poor engineer or outmoded engineering; the work and the people responsible for it are the butt of the joke:

(a) After drawing on earlier relay circuit, says 'O.K., let's stop fooling around,' and draws the very simple diagram of today's device.
(b) 'The picture of the Line Finder has an interesting error—it's printed sideways, and since the function of gravity to restore the switch is a vital part of it, the Line Finder as pictured wouldn't work very well.'
(c) 'You could tell when a line was busy in those days ... there was a wire in the jack.'

This apparently harmless humor, which appreciates sophistication, difficulty, complexity of purpose coupled with speed, elegance, simplicity of design and construction, can be a source of pleasure in engineering or any other science. Such humor also heightens awareness of the technically competent class with which one wants to identify as against the class of incompetents one wants to avoid. Given a somewhat different emphasis, however, jokes of this type also reflect the way in which some professors made difficulty and competition ends in themselves in order to 'separate the men from the boys.' With such stress on the rational and technical and on competition for grades rather than on comprehensive understanding, the most creative and sensitive students opt out; those who recognize and accept the game continue (Snyder, 1973).

Humor also reflected the great disdain of some professors for the social sciences:

(d) 'Scientists and engineers stand on the shoulders of giants. Social scientists stand on their faces.'

(2) Although engineering education apparently seeks to separate technology from its social context, social relations are very relevant to today's engineer/managers. I found that appropriate social values and behavior were often conveyed informally through classroom humor. In this second most frequent category of jokes (26 per cent), the status of engineers was elevated over that of students, workers, ghetto dwellers, and, most often, women:

(e) 'A girl in (M) dorm wanted help with her homework. She called guys, either in her class—or one year ahead. [Laughter] She'd say, "Where were we when we were cut off, wasn't it on problem three?" The guy would go along with this usually. Once she got a phone hacker. By hitting the button a number of times, you could tell which lines in the dorm were busy ... He did this while talking to her about 20 minutes, and only one other lines was consistently busy. [By a simple calculation] you can get the room number from the phone number. So he says, 'By the way, how are things in 543?"

(f) 'Multiple switchboards determine how long an operator's arms have to be. [The Institute] used to have operators; when they walked down the hall their knuckles would drag the floor. They could serve 700 jacks depending on their position.'

Workers, often black, were referred to as 'coolies':

Comment after a tour of a switching system located in a black neighborhood, which was soon to be automated with the Electronic Switching System: 'You may have noticed coolies running ... here and there "tweaking" [the system], and that's an expensive operation.'

(The workers, many of them minority men, faced a 60–80 per cent reduction rate after the change, according to a guide.)

(g) Same tour: 'Shall we take a bus or an armored car to get there?'

(3) Third in frequency (17 per cent) were jokes about morality or ethics—bluntly, about how to 'rip off.'

(h) About computers: 'In the telephone, speed doesn't matter that much. Depends on who you're competing with. And accuracy—it's fixed so that the subscriber will believe it's him.'
(i) Joking references to stolen equipment.

Professors' jokes elevate the status of those who can break the rules and get away with it.

(4) Last in frequency (13 per cent) were jokes drawing some analogy between machine and body function, or simply a reference to such functions, most often scatalogical.

(j) The early version of an ESS (Electronic Switching System) looked like a well-built outhouse.'
(k) Answer to a question: 'Weelll, this is all men's room hearsay ... '
(l) You don't know when transistors are unhappy. Relays smell when they're unhappy'
(m) Reference to timing the load of calls and flush toilets: 'We all know that water pressure is correlated with the time of TV commercials.'

Professors' jokes transmit values, warning the students what to avoid and what to emulate, approving the higher status and benefits of mental work, particularly of an abstract or scientific nature. Poking fun at the body and its functions may be the other side of this coin; putting down the body elevates the mind.

Among the several approaches to the analysis of humor, LaFave's (1974) seemed most relevant to these data. His model explains the butt of a joke as opponent or competitor. The Marxist critique of capitalism more readily explains why workers or honesty might be viewed as opponents. The concept of a reserve labor army, which demands a divided work force such as that observed in the research on technological displacement, might explain the tendency to further subordinate women and minorities. But for understanding the elevation of abstraction and technical competence or putting down the body, we must look elsewhere—to the cult and culture of technology itself.

MIND/BODY DUALISMS: WOMEN, WORKPLACE AND MACHINE

In the industrialized world, technology fused with science produces a new notion of the Good, a technical ideology held most strongly by engineers (Gouldner, 1976). Technical skills compete with skills of nurturance and responsiveness to the needs of others (Rossi, 1965), and the competition is pretty one-sided. Technical expertise is also closely related to what some consider modern day's most exciting and engrossing work, such as the design and development of advanced weapons systems. This work of protection and defense is most highly rewarded. But there are costs as well. Marcuse (1964), suggests that for technical rationality to 'work' (as an ideology to shore up hierarchy in social relations) it must be divorced from sexuality:

'True knowledge and reason demand domination over—if not liberation from—the senses.... The link between reason and sexuality or eroticism is broken; scientific rationality dominates. As nature is scientifically comprehended and mastered ... the rational hierarchy merges with the social one.' (p. 166).

The question, of course, is why this seems necessarily so, and why someone is willing to pay such a price. My exploratory work can only suggest areas for more thorough or systematic inquiry into such dualisms, their origins and meaning.

The research and observations presented here highlight strong elements of mind/body dualism in the culture of engineering. Such dualism also seems firmly linked to a preference for clearly defined and hierarchical relationships such as those found in the organization of industrial work. In Western society, the highest places in a social hierarchy are not held by those with qualities of the divine, but by those with qualities defined as scientific or technological rationality. The lowest places, the least rewards to those with qualities of the womanly—nurturance, routine maintenance, intimacy, sensuality, social and emotional complexity. Possible origins of such dualisms are suggested by some to correspond to changes in social organization, such as increased fertility, women's subordination and the separation of man from woman and child (Nielson, 1978; Stanley, 1980; and for speculations relating to military institutions, see Hacker, B., 1977.) Ideological justifications for such significant social transformations can be found in both myth and religion. Lewis Mumford (1970, p. 28), for example, traces the 'deity that presided over the new religion and the new mechanical world picture' of the sixteenth and seventeenth centuries to the ancient 'Atum-Re, the self-created Sun, who out of his own semen had created the universe and all its subordinate deities ... without the aid of the female principle.'

Scatalogical humor, an almost exclusively male prerogative in modern society, may further reflect the evolution of men's concern for increasing female fertility during these transformations, and their separation from women and children. Philosophical and anthropological literature on scatological jokes and myths suggest these also reflect man's concern with his creativity and sexuality, and the anxiety about his minimal role in reproduction. Dundes (1962) also discusses male envy of pregnancy and childbirth as a source of male creativity. His data on excretory myths offer examples of male fantasies of anal birth. These myths, he found, serve a similar function:

'The creator is able to create without reference to women. Whether a male creator spins material, molds clay, lays an egg, fabricates from mucous or epidermal tissue or dives for fecal mud, the psychological motive is the same ..., a flaunting of anal creativity without the participation of women.' (p. 1046).

In the fields of philosophy and science, both al-Hibri (1981) and Keller (1980) illuminate this male desire for generative power, the power to reproduce without women's participation. The mind is the instrument of creation; woman has been identified with the body. Today, as well, the mind is clearly superior to the body, which is dumb and sexy, unpredictable, and much in need of discipline and control.

Persistent mind/body dualism may well be the root of a central concern of present-day socialist analysis of technology (Braverman, 1974), the separation of mind and hand in the labor process as management transfers craft knowledge to machines run by cheaper and less skilled hands. But the separation of mind from body followed the earlier social separation of man from woman and child. Socialist analysis may need a more extensive historical approach to integrate questions of women's place, and of sexuality, with the inquiry into the degradation of labor.

I believe such dualisms help explain both technological displacement as it varies by race and sex as well as class, and female exclusion in the culture of engineering. In Western society, it is a technological rather than a religious ideology which justifies the existing order. In the everyday lives of engineering/management, and in the early lives of leaders in élite engineering education, we see reflections of man/woman and mind/body dualisms, related to strong notions about hierarchy in the world of work.

Material conditions leading to a patriarchal ideology in history may parallel socialization experiences of both the engineering and the humanities faculty interviewed. Boys are separated from girls; both learn that females have babies and therefore have a closer link with nature. Women are viewed as better suited to childrearing as well as childbearing than are men. Men benefit by relief from child care, by free home and self maintenance, and by lack of competition for better jobs in the paid market (Sokoloff, 1980; Brown, 1979).

As Chodorow (1974) suggests, when only women do the parenting, boys learn to develop skills of cognitive control rather than of nurturance, intimacy, and the maintenance of daily life. They also learn to believe the former set of skills are more valuable than the latter; those who protect and provide for the others deserve a greater share of goods and services than do the protected.

Men on the engineering faculty shared with those in the humanities this general alienation from women, centering on reproduction, denial or suppression of intimacy in social relations, and a desire to order the natural world. In childhood, however, men in the humanities faculty may have learned to accept conflict as naturally inherent in intimate social relations. But now they showed more concern than engineering faculty over the power and unpredictability of women. This is a pattern described Fatima Mernissi (1975) in Muslim societies—a fear of and respect for the power of women's sexuality, which, in those societies, is dealt with firmly and directly. This view of women does not seem to predominate in Western culture, where the individual is expected to control her/his own sexuality. Perhaps the engineering faculty epitomizes this more peculiarly Western view, one which places ever greater emphasis on the man alone, and his ability for rational self control. Whereas men in the humanities in this research may have expressed concern for the unpredictability of female sexuality, the engineering faculty by comparison seemed more concerned with their own.

The men who chose engineering had early life experiences which emphasized aloneness, which allowed them greater distance from intimacy or the pleasures and dangers of 'mixing it up' with other people. Many became fascinated instead with things, and how they worked. These experiences heightened the value placed on abstraction and control over the natural— women, reproduction, emotions, intimacy, sensuality, their own physical selves. It is only the body, however, which cannot be literally distanced to obtain such control.

Later in life—here, from observation in the classroom as well as interviews—engineers tended to learn that other men also, or the work and qualities they represent, such as blacks, workers (Adamson, 1980), social scientists, and finally even those in some fields of engineering, have womanly characteristics. Rather than being clean, hard, abstract, such non-technical men or their activities show characteristics of emotionality, sensuality, or interest and skill in social complexity. A technological ideology justifies control over these other men as well, which in its turn brings greater reward for those with the skills of greatest abstraction, and greatest technical competence. Social hierarchy along these dimensions appears the most rational way to organize people to accomplish work. This is a fairly well articulated ideology of technology, as expressed by the engineering faculty in this study.

Gouldner (1976), however, in his work on ideology and technology, pictures a paleosymbolic system 'older and earlier' than ideology. Preceding a publicly articulated ideology, the paleosymbolic, the 'old snake brain' of beliefs and symbols, rests on a more private kind of communication. Its language is learned in childhood, linked 'to [the] provision of gratification and security for the self of the learner, and hence with the most elemental system of affects.' This language may generally only be spoken 'to intimates in private settings,' or among those presumed to share similar interests (pp. 224–225).

Gouldner's analysis is applied to the way management's needs shape the ideology of technology. But what I perceived among both engineering/managers and the way they viewed women workers, and what I saw in the institute, was an 'old snake brain' of partriarchal beliefs, justifying male dominance. These beliefs underlie the new articulated ideology of technology, and may become more visible as the technological base and workforce of industry are being substantially transformed.

A challenge to the technological world view may very well be perceived as an attack on reason itself. But such challenges—women's entry into engineering or the crafts, for example—may bring to light more of the 'paleosymbolic' elements beneath a technological ideology.[4]

These elements bode well neither for women nor, it appears, for the fruits of engineering, which may be shaped in ways many engineers themselves would not want to see (Garson, 1977; Melman, 1970; Hoos, 1972).

Such partriarchal elements in technology as they affect women, work, and workplace need also be to explored in relation to capitalism, research I am pursuing for their internal contradictions, as well as for the convergences and contradictions of the two systems. For example increasing specialization and hierarchy have been linked to declining productivity and technical malfunction, as the numbers of organizational levels increase and with them the distances between engineer/managers and the workers and machines they must coordinate. Within engineering, automation produces demands which may lead to deskilling, now and in the near future (Hacker, 1980). These changes may provide new

---

[4] Like scatological myths and humor, popular culture and even everyday conversation about technology often reflect a masculine concern for creativity and reproduction. Florman's work (1976) reveals that sexuality and reproductive creativity are often channeled toward the machine, with metaphors of potency, creation of 'new forms' of life, feelings of love etc. The very phallic imagery of defence technology is a cliché, as in a film by the aerospace giant, McDonnell–Douglas: 'We Bring Technology To Life!' which portrays repeated views of rockets being erected and slow-motion shots of ejection. This portrayal parallels an engineer's comment about the 'drive' introduced into electrical engineering by its increasingly tight links with industry, as 'the electric penis approach.' If we have here some elements of the patriarchal desire to create 'without the participation of the female principle' that Mumford (1970) noted, we can hardly wonder that women are hard-pressed to enter and remain in blue-collar crafts or technical professions such as engineering.

conditions, perhaps new opportunities, for women. As Joan Acker (1980) tells us in her review of the literature on sex stratification:

'The interesting and potentially useful questions are not how individuals get into certain slots, but how the structure itself is formed and what its changing contours are' (p. 29).

My central concern is to develop a framework that will help us understand those changing contours and how they will affect women, technology, and the workplace. The work of both Marxists and radical feminists can give us valuable insights. If this research approach aids us to reduce the imbalance of power between men and women, and to reverse the process of social hierarchy, it may also help transform the shape and direction of our current technological endeavors, our troubled relationships with others, with the natural world, and with our own physical, erotic selves.

REFERENCES

Adamson, Lesley. 1980. More to lose than their chains. *New Internationalist* **89,** 7–9.
Acker, Joan. 1980. Women and stratification: a review of recent literature. *Contemporary Sociology* **9,** 25–39.
Braverman, Harry. 1974. *Labor and Monopoly Capital.* Monthly Review Press, New York.
Brown, Carol. 1979. The political economy of sexual inequality. Paper presented at annual meeting of the Society for the Study of Social Problems, Boston.
Christoffel, Tom and Kaufer, Katherine. 1970. The political economy of male chauvinism. In: Christoffel, Tom Finkelhor, David and Gilbarg, Dan, eds. *Up Against the American Myth*, Holt, Rinehart and Winston, New York.
Chodorow, Nancy. 1974. Family structure and feminine personality. In: Rosaldo, Michelle Zimbalist and Lamphere, Louise, eds. *Women, Culture and Society.* Stanford University Press, California.
Dundes, Alan. 1962. Earthdiver: creation of the mythopoeic male. *American Anthopologist* **64,** 1032–1051.
Feldberg, Roslyn and Glenn, Evelyn Nakano. 1980. Effects of technological change on clerical work. Paper presented at annual meetings of the American Sociological Association, New York.
Florman, Samuel. 1976. *The Existential Pleasures of Engineering.* St. Martin's Press, New York.
Garson, Barbara. 1977. *All the Livelong Day.* Penguin Books, New York.
Gouldner, Alvin. 1976. *Dialectic of Ideology and Technology.* Seaburg Press, New York.
Hacker, Barton. 1977. The prevalence of war and the oppression of women: an essay on armies and the origin of the state. Paper presented to the Conference on Women and Power, University of Maryland.
Hacker, Sally. 1977. Farming out the home: women and agribusiness. *The Second Wave* **5,** 38–49.
Hacker, Sally. 1978. Man and humanism: language, gender and power. *Humanity and Society* **2,** 62–78.
Hacker, Sally. 1979. Sex stratification, technology and organizational change: a longitudinal case study of AT & T. *Social Problems* **26** (5), 539–557.
Hacker, Sally. 1980. The automated and the automaters: human and social costs of automation. Paper presented at annual meetings of the International Federation of Automatic Control, Rabat, Morocco. (Forthcoming *Proceedings.* Pergamon, New York).
Hartmann, Heidi. 1976. Capitalism, patriarchy and job segregation by sex. In: Blaxall, Martha and Regan, Barbara, eds. *Women and the Workplace.* University of Chicago Press.
al-Hibri, Azizah. 1981. Capitalism is an advanced state of patriarchy: but Marxism is not feminism. In: Sargent, Lydia, ed. *Women and Revolution.* South End Press, Boston.
Hoos, Ida. 1972. *Systems Analysis in Public Policy.* University of California Press, Berkeley.
Keller, Evelyn Fox. 1980. Baconian science: a hermaphroditic birth. *Philosophical Forum* **XI,** (3).
LaFave, Lawrence, Haddod, Jay and Marshall, Nancy. 1974. Human judgments as a function of identification classes. *Sociology and Social Research* **58** (2), 184–194.
Marcuse, Herbert. 1964. *One Dimensional Man.* Beacon Press, Boston.
Melman, Seymour. 1970. *Pentagon Capitalism.* McGraw Hill, New York.
Mernissi, Fatima. 1975. *Beyond the Veil.* Schenkman, Cambridge, Mass.
Mumford, Lewis. 1970. *The Myth of the Machine: the Pentagon of power.* Harcourt, Brace, Jovanovich, New York.
Nielsen, Joyce. 1978. *Sex in Society.* Wadsworth, Belmont, Calif.
Northwestern Bell Telephone Company. 1973. *Job Descriptions.* Des Moines, Iowa.
Ott, Mary Diederich and Reese, Nancy A. 1975. *Women in Engineering.* Cornell University Press, Ithaca, New York.
Rossi, Alice. 1965. Barriers to the career choice of engineering, medicine or science among American women. In: Van Aken, Jacquelyn and Carol, eds. *MIT Symposium on American Women in Science and Engineering, 1964: Women in the Scientific Professions.* MIT Press, Cambridge, Mass.

Snyder, Ben. 1973. *The Hidden Curriculum.* MIT Press, Cambridge, Mass.

Sokoloff, Natalie. 1980. *Between Money and Love: the dialectics of women's home and market work.* Praeger, New York.

Stanley, Autumn. 1980. Daughters of Ceres: women inventors in agriculture. Paper presented at annual meetings of the National Women's Studies Association, Bloomington, Indiana. (See also Stanley, this issue of WSIQ).

Women's Studies Int. Quart., Vol. 4, No. 3, pp. 355–367, 1981.
Printed in Great Britain.

0148–0685/81/030355–13$02.00/0
Pergamon Press Ltd.

TECHNOLOGY AND THE FUTURE OF WOMEN: HAVEN'T WE MET SOMEWHERE BEFORE?

JAN ZIMMERMAN

201 East Twelfth Street, New York, NY 10003, 212–475–4630

Synopsis—Advanced technology is popularly perceived as a harbinger of progress. However, this essay argues that for women such progress often results in the reinforcement of traditional economic and social roles. The paper examines four technological areas—computers, communications, energy production, and genetic engineering—which will have an enormous impact on women's lives in the next 20 years.

Analyzing the encoding of old values in these new technologies, the author concludes that political control of technological development is imperative for women. Otherwise, women will be condemned, like the Red Queen in *Alice in Wonderland*, to run faster and faster to stay in the same place.

Security Pacific Bank commercials[1] tantalize us with glimpses of tomorrow: cities beneath the sea, factories in outer space, computers in the home, and instant communications to everywhere. Reminding us 'that people will always need each other,' the bank commits itself to those who are 'looking forward.' But feminists need to examine seriously this and other forward-looking visions, for at close inspection the glittering vistas of the future have a disquieting resemblance to the past.

New technologies—computers, communication networks, energy production, genetic engineering—have the potential of improving women's lives if, and only if, women gain political and financial control over the development and implementation of these inventions. Without such control, women will find themselves replaying a familiar scenario in which new technologies serve to reinforce old values. Since the 'driver' of economic growth (productivity) in Western capitalism has always been new technology (Merchant, 1980, Samuelson, 1980), women must confront squarely this economic function of technological development before they can improve their own economic status. To avoid the struggle with technology is to condemn women to their history. Or, as former U.S. astronaut James Lovell so succinctly expressed it, 'We will fly women into space and use them the same way we use them on earth—for the same purpose.'[2]

It would be impossible to catalog exhaustively the impacts of all new technologies on women's lives. Therefore, this essay will consider four of those which may have a dramatic impact on the operating conditions of women's lives, but minimal or negative effects on their economic and social roles. These technologies are discussed primarily in terms of their effects on Western, middle class women.

LE PLUS ÇA CHANGE, LE PLUS C'EST LA MÊME CHOSE

The loss of the future is too remote and intangible for the woman struggling with day-to-day existence to contemplate. Seeking economic and psychic survival in a discriminatory

---

[1] Presented on television stations in Southern California, Summer–Fall 1980.
[2] Quoted in Kazickas and Sherr, 1980. *The Woman's Calendar for 1980.*

environment, in a recessionary and inflationary economy, with half-to-all the household earnings increasingly on her shoulders, the weight of housekeeping on her feet and two children tugging at her apron strings—the last thing today's woman has time to worry about is tomorrow.

Given the strength of capitalism in Western industrialized nations, it is improbable that social forces will succeed in radically altering women's economic and cultural roles within the 20-year time frame that will bring these new technologies to fruition. In all likelihood the immediate future will see women continuing to fulfil the economic roles in which they have been exploitatively cast:

(1) Traditionally women have been used as surplus labor to provide high quality work at low pay in industries which demand temporary or part-time workers (Howe, 1977).

(2) Women's unpaid labor in home- and child-care is invisible in the Gross National Product and thus considered non-essential; the production role of women at home is limited to the production of children.

(3) In advanced capitalism women's role is to balance male-powered production with female-driven consumption. As economist John Galbraith described it, 'the decisive contribution of women in the developed industrial society is . . . overwhelmingly to facilitate continuing a more or less unlimited increase in consumption' (Galbraith, 1967, p. 33).

(4) Women serve as the object of social violence: they are the employees on the bottom of the totem pole (particularly black women), the physical victims of radiation, chemical and environmental pollution. They are the human third of war booty (the rape portion of rape, pillage, and plunder) and constantly fight a guerrilla battle against rapists and wife-beaters.

New technologies which promise liberation may offer women only these same roles to play in the social drama of tomorrow. Careful consideration of these technologies—computers, communications, energy production, and genetic engineering—is thus necessary, since they may present us with unexpected benefits to be reaped or terrify us with nightmares of the only-to-be-expected. The difference will depend on the issue of technological control.

'MA'AM, THERE'S A COMPUTER IN YOUR GARDEN'

The microprocessor chip, with all its applications, undoubtedly will have the most extensive near-term impact on technological development of any invention now on the market. Essentially, a microprocessor chip is a computer cookie, a bite-sized adding machine, which can be combined with other devices to perform a variety of functions requiring computation, memory, or comparison. These chips, generally less than $1'' \times \frac{1}{4}'' \times \frac{1}{4}''$ and sometimes even smaller, are nothing more than electronic circuits compressed to a very small size. The electronic components used in the room-sized Univac computers of the 1950's now fit in the palm of a child's hand.

This small size means not only the capability of building smaller computers, but also the capability of turning other devices into 'intelligent' machines. Microprocessors can be installed easily into the dumbest of devices, such as ovens, televisions and cars. Microwave ovens can be programmed to turn on, defrost, cook and brown a roast; a television set can become a Star Trek war game; a car dashboard can display the firing sequences of pistons and remember oil changes; and a home computer, plugged into regular electric sockets, can be programmed to turn on and off lights, home security devices, heating units and the morning coffee maker.

Microprocessors have one other essential attribute: they are cheap. In the economy of electronic technology, anything that's cheap gets used, and the more it's used, the cheaper it gets. The rapid development of the hand-held calculator, now no larger than a credit card, and its plummeting cost, from over $100 to under $10 in less than 5 years, is the quintessential classic example.

The ubiquitous chip has some profound implications for the nature of women's lives at home and at work. At home the chips mean expanded use of relatively low cost personal computers. Currently priced anywhere from $700 at Radio Shack to several thousand dollars for more sophisticated versions, computers are now purchased as a luxury or recreational item by hobbyists and by the middle and upper classes. But as costs go down and ease of use goes up—Mattel Toy Company is now marketing 'Intellivision'[3]—computers will become a necessity for access to information. By the year 2000 living without a computer, in a state of information poverty, will effectively exclude people from many day-to-day activities in society and will certainly exclude them from power.

On a simple convenience level, users will insert pre-packaged programs to monitor home systems for energy-saving purposes, to maintain household accounts and records, and to provide entertainment; students will use computers to do homework, writers to prepare books and letters, household members to leave messages and reminders for one another. The real power of microprocessor, however, lies beyond their use as a new consumer goodie within the home; it lies in their connection to external services:

—Utility companies are now experimenting with computers to monitor and control energy usage, sending signals over power lines to turn appliances on and off (Shaffer, 1980).

—Banks in New York City and Columbus, Ohio, are testing an extension of electronic funds transfer (EFT) to determine the feasibility of using home computers and push-button phones to pay bills and conduct all banking transactions (Banking From Home, 1980).

—The British are experimenting with 'Prestel,' a television-displayed 'viewdata' service which provides subscribers with a hand-held keypad to request computer data-based travel schedules, statistical indicators, and entertainment guides at home (Learn More From Your TV Read It, 1980).

—Other services, such as library reference, news, and shopping are also in experimental use.

In the workplace, there are even more changes underway. The automated office of the future, with its word processors, automatic typewriters and electronic mail systems, will need fewer and fewer workers with secretarial skills, a workforce which is 99 per cent female in the U.S. (Howe, 1977). Word processors and keypunchers (the worker equals the machine) will evolve as 'women's jobs'; both involve routine, keyboard-based data entry, the former onto a TV screen, the latter onto punched cards.

When direct voice-to-computer transmission becomes practical and cost-efficient for extensive business use in 15–20 years, even those jobs will disappear, along with those of

---

[3] Radio Shack, a nationwide chain, advertises extensively in the United States; Mattel's products are found on the shelves of major department stores.

telephone operators and airline reservation agents. It is already possible to 'talk-back to your television set,' if it has been 'trained' to commands from your voice to change channels or turn off.

Computers will generate growth in the workforce in such areas as programming, system maintenance, and engineering. Only one of these jobs, however, is likely to become women's work—programming. A recent issue of *Computer World* described how technological advances in high-level computer languages and structured programming will result in the 'de-skilling' of yesterday's 'shining knights of programming' (Schultz, 1980). Tomorrow's programmers will be 'seen as clerical workers and enjoy less prestige.' The article notes that 'these lower paid workers are usually more adaptable to factory-style production environments,' easing the task of software managers who await software systems that will generate other software systems, 'reducing the need for human programmers to almost nothing.' The same issue of the magazine carried another article detailing a grant awarded to the University of Texas at Austin by the National Science Foundation to train women in computer science, primarily to become programmers' (Project Opens Computer Science Jobs to Women, 1980).

Professionals in other fields will also feel the impact of the microprocessor revolution. Everyone from stockbrokers to social workers, from advertising agents to jounalists, everyone who needs access to information will routinely use a computer. Computer/communication interfaces will make it simple to do such work from home. The same telephone lines that make 'terminal-to-terminal' mail delivery possible, make it possible for a worker to carry home a terminal that can exchange information with a distant office base.

On the one hand, working at home could be a tremendous boon: work could be available to the physically handicapped, to those in rural areas, to those without access to cheap, convenient transportation. Working with computers at home could reduce gasoline consumption, freeway congestion, and air pollution, and could eliminate thousands of hours of wasted commuting time. It could provide work-hour flexibility and an opportunity for greater involvement in child-rearing by both parents.

Or, it may, as Alvin Toffler quotes with a straight face in his new book, *The Third Wave*, allow 'married secretaries caring for small children at home to continue to work' (Toffler, 1980). Computers at home could allow women, that is, to do not one, but two jobs in their cozy, rose-covered, picket-fenced, white frame, electronic bungalows.

One of the greatest advantages of computer information systems is their capacity for rapid access to statistical data, bibliographies, and references. New database services, which charge users according to the length of computer time used, have sprung up world-wide. Three of the largest are run by System Development Corporation (ORBIT), Lockheed (DIALOG) and the U.S. Department of Commerce National Technical Information Service (NTIS). These services, available by mail or phone, provide information on agriculture and energy, medicine, law, physics, and social science; they have databases for accountants, educators and administrators, but none of them has a database on women. (As of September 1980, Lockheed was considering opening a file on *Women's Studies Abstracts*, but expected it would be a year before the service was on-line).

Gathering information on women's issues requires a costly and time-consuming search of many files within one of these systems. Obviously, without control over data entry, women will find the information potential of computers unsatisfactory for their needs. The power of naming, which has been well documented in feminist literature (Griffin, 1978; Daly, 1978), holds true as much for numbers as for words. Women must determine which questions should be aksed, which data collected, which categories used. Without the power to validate their statistical existence, women become phantom figures in the war of numbers. To date, only one effort to use computers to meet women's real needs has been attempted: the Feminist Computer Technology Project, initiated at the National Women's Studies Association Conference in 1979 (Densmore, 1979), seeks to create a network of women working with computer technology for resource and information sharing.[4]

In summary, women could use computers to: ease housekeeping responsibilities, reduce time spent running errands, lower transportation and energy costs, encourage the adoption of flexible working hours; support shared parenting responsibilities, and gain access to information resources crucial to political change (Densmore, 1978). Or computers could use women, just as other technologies have. They could push women into even more alienating, low-paying jobs or out of the workplace altogether; they could double women's bind to the home, and make it impossible for women to acquire control over the information being used by others to make decisions about women's lives.

Even those companies, like Atari, which recognize that new social roles for women will configure a new market structure, assume that computers must be marketed by color and decorator styling to appeal to women (Rosenthal, 1980). The difference between these two sets of options lies clearly in the control of the technology.

'THE LAST THING MY WIFE NEEDS IS A SATELLITE, SHE TALKS ON THE PHONE TOO MUCH ALREADY.'[5]

Women do not fare much better with communications technology than they do with computers. Science fiction fantasies of wristwatch-to-satellite communication services can quickly become nightmares for women. ('Mommy, wherever you are, come get me. The Cub Scout meeting's over.') Multi-channel television capacity through optical fiber or improved cable systems can offer the false choice of six syndicated TV shows, five Hollywood-style movies, four sporting events, and three versions of the news. World-wide picturephone service offers equally uncertain benefits to women (does it help to talk to London if there isn't time to talk to the people across the street?). These commercially controlled systems will continue to violate any promise for women as long as programming (content) remains outside of women's hands and as long as economic accessibility (form) determines the use of sophisticated communications technology.

Yet these systems do have the potential to meet women's need to utilize the capacity of the media to validate experience and define reality. Satellite communication could be used to hold meetings in rural areas or to link chapters of nationwide organizations in different cities for teleconferences. With access to satellites, cable systems, and video disk/cassette distribution networks, women could communicate their needs, concerns, and points of view to each other and to the world audience (Zimmerman, 1977). Cable technologies could provide two-way interactive communications for national town meetings or alternative question-and-answer news conferences on women's issues.

Regardless of the technology, women's programming lacks funding sources, an aggregated market of financially-able subscribers, or interested sponsors. Instead, Walt Disney Enterprises uses Bell Laboratories' advanced optical fiber system for increased telephone

---

[4] The Feminist Computer Technology Project is now being directed by Elisabeth Reinhardt of Erin Information Systems, San Diego, Calif.

[5] Comment made to author at NASA conference on Public Service Communications Satellites, March 29, 1977.

capacity at Disneyworld (MacFadyen, 1980); satellites are used to transmit Home Box Office movies, sporting events (Hill, 1978), and news (Margulies, 1979) to cable systems around the country; and Xerox, IBM, and Satellite Business Systems compete aggressively for the integrated communication service market represented by multinational corporations (*Behind AT&T's Change at the Top*, 1978; Caswell, 1978; Xerox, 1979).

Direct satellite-to-home broadcasting may relax some of the stringency of this scenario. Both the Japanese and the Canadians are currently testing such technology, leading to predictions of commercial viability by the end of the century. In this sytem, a viewer places an 18″ diameter satellite receiving dish on top of a TV set, instead of a regular antenna, to pick up a wide range of signals generated from many different points and relayed by an orbiting satellite to the viewer's terminal. While this service would eliminate the communications brokering now done by networks, women will still have to gain access to production equipment and to the funds needed to 'uplink' their programs to a satellite in the first place.

If the past is any indicator, women will have a difficult time altering the nature of media accessibility. To date they have had only minor success in changing patterns of employment in the media, ending sex-role stereotyping in programming, or increasing coverage of women's news. Because of the complexities of hardware development and regulatory processes, women frequently are shut out of access to communications systems during the planning stages, long before the public has been informed of new technical developments. Once locked into place through physical design, financing, and regulatory contraints, hardware systems are difficult to change. Effective access requires women to become involved in communications planning at the inception of new technologies.

Two of the most innovative efforts to gain technological access for women have involved satellites. The first, the National Women's Agenda Satellite Services Project, sought to use a government-owned, experimental satellite to connect 100 women's organizations in six cities around the United States. In 1977 the Agenda received 'experimenter' status from the National Aeronautics and Space Administration (NASA) to use CTS, a joint Canadian/American satellite for audio teleconferencing, telex, facsimile, and data transmission (the same services Xerox, IBM, and Satellite Business Systems will provide their multinational customers). Just prior to their first demonstration, the Agenda was forced off the satellite by NASA for refusing conditions that the women not discuss lesbianism and abortion via satellite (Zimmerman, 1978).[6]

In a second extraordinary demonstration of how women would use advanced telecommunications, the Women's Institute for Freedom of the Press, based in Washington, D.C., received a grant from the U.S. International Communications Agency to produce an international teleconference by satellite for the United Nations Mid-Decade World Conference of Women in Copenhagen in July 1980. Two closed-circuit satellite teleconferences were held, linking women in Copenhagen to women in Minneapolis, Houston, Los Angeles, Boston, Atlanta, and Washington, D.C., using the satellite facilities of the Corporation for Public Broadcasting in the United States (Allen, 1980). The utility of the system was limited only by lack of access to full broadcast services: to participate women had to assemble at local public television stations, thus reducing the number of viewers. But contrast this effort with the minimal coverage of the conference provided by major print,

---

[6] The author initiated and directed this project.

radio and television services. When it did occur, mass media coverage was negative and distorted, reporting only the conflicts in Copenhagen (Morgan, 1980).

Cable systems combined with computers offer options for several non-programming services, such as reference, news and shopping. Viewers could 'dial up' and display reference materials from the public library's information retrieval system, read their daily newspaper, or purchase items off a video selection list, all by using either telephone lines or a special keypad for two-way communication.

The QUBE experiment in Columbus, Ohio, tested the use of a keypad response device with cable television to determine viewer interaction levels for 'straw polls' on local political issues, game shows, and educational programs (Margulies, 1977). A keypad can also be used with a broadcast signal, in a variation of the 'closed captioned' Teletext system used by the hearing-impaired. (The British Prestel service described above uses this technology.) Zenith has just demonstrated a television set which can handle an incoming telephone call and which eventually will allow two-way connection to viewdata systems (*TV With a Phone*, 1980).

But behind the glory of saturation video lies a market-conscious consumer economy. Given demographic data on household composition as part of the subscription process, cable companies could sell a highly selected audience to advertisers, even more precisely than broadcasters now sell their program audiences (Smythe, 1976). Those readers with video visions of 1984 dancing like sugarplums in their heads may contemplate the routing of news information based on demographics, with different audiences receiving pre-selected material or items written according to a pre-determined slant, resulting in such fragmentation of information that no one knows what is happening, what is real.

At first glance video shopping and banking appear to save time, money, and energy for women, who consistently are required to perform these household support tasks. However, the substitution of electronic communication for face-to-face contact may re-isolate women in the home, scattering their still nascent organizational efforts, reducing their opportunities to gain information about the ouside world, and alienating them from the direct experience which has been a source of female strength.

With the impetus of an oil shortage, it is no surprise to find communications systems touted as a non-polluting, energy efficient alternative to transportation. As these telecommunications services proliferate, fostered by the twin forces of increased computing power and decreased commuting power, women may find themselves once again prisoners of gilded suburban cages, their feet bound by copper cable, optical fiber, and the invisible chains of electromagnetic waves.

'TRY TELLING THE LADY SHE'LL HAVE TO START WASHING BY HAND.'[7]

There is no question that the industrialized nations consume far more than their share of the energy pie: the 'rich' nations with less than one-third of the world's population use more than three-quarters of the world's energy resources (Schumacher, 1973). There is no question that the consumer economy drives up the use of electrical energy for extraneous purposes to meet artificially created demands, e.g. electric toothbrushes. But there is a question when it comes to energy politics—*qui bono*? Who will benefit from the alternative energy sources, coal gasification, synfuel, and oil shale, now being funded by the United States government?

---

[7] Reprinted in the leaflet *Growthmania* by Donna Warnock, 1979a.

Who will suffer most from the high costs of energy—the rich or the poor (two-thirds of whom are women)? Who will conserve—large-scale businesses or households?

In a search for equality, job parity, and personal growth, women need to have the time and personal energy to devote to political action, education, and themselves. For a woman holding down two full-time jobs, one at the paid workplace and one at home, time- and labor-saving devices serve a crucial need. Simple things, like the access to a car, become essentials. Margaret McCormack of the California Office of Appropriate Technology expresses a working mother's lifestyle succinctly:

'I recall watching college students bury a gas guzzling car on Earth Day '70 thinking that they had never raced in such a car to an emergency ward on the other side of town at 3 a.m. with one feverish baby in the front seat and its healthy sibling sleeping in the back seat. Nor did they have the harried daily routines of driving miles in one direction to the only available childcare center, miles in another direction to get to work, back to the center before it closed, and off in yet another direction to pick up some food for dinner. Nor had they probably ever tried using bicycles to shop or do laundry with two kids in tow.' (McCormack, 1977 p. 18)

One utility consortium, self-described as 'investor-owned electric light and power companies' (Warnock, 1979a) ran an advertisement pleading for public support to build new generating facilities. The advertisement, with the headline at the top of this section, showed a woman defending her washing machine—as well she should. How many working mothers have the time to wash by hand? How many mothers want a return to all-cotton, all-iron clothes? How many want a solar drier, so they can hang out the clothes and bring them in? Who is being asked to wash a day's worth of dishes for six by hand? To spend 4 hours cooking dinner in the solar oven on the roof? Recent surveys show that very few husbands in the United States provide any meaningful household help (Bose, 1979; Greene, 1980). To sort out which potential energy conservation and generation schemes hold promise for women, it is critical to eliminate those systems which present either labor-intensive or health-hazardous costs as mandatory trade-offs to the benefit of lower prices.

Proposals for alternative energy sources are now in more abundant supply than any fossil fuel. Some are decentralized, others centralized; some capital-intensive, some labor-intensive. Proposals for decentralized energy production encompass solar, wind, and mechanical devices, as well as changes in building siting and construction. Simple passive solar systems can result in hot water heating and home-heating in temperate climates at relatively low cost. Such devices could reduce energy costs to consumers at minimal cost of time and labor beyond installation. But other decentralized systems, such as home methane digesters or pedal-power, are not much of a boon to a woman who would like to have personal energy to expend beyond sheer survival.

Some forms of decentralized energy production, for example, wind and water mills, may work in rural areas but are difficult to implement in an urban environment, though not impossible. Changes in building codes and use of natural forces (winds, tides, geothermal springs) depend on location and at least regional or neighborhood-wide generating systems for efficiency. Most forms of decentralized production have been opposed by large and powerful monopoly utilities, whose primary allegiance is to their investors, not their customers. As they devise means to profit from the use of alternative energy sources, the utilities fequently turn from adversaries to advocates (Reece, 1980).

The major alternatives to oil that are being promoted in the Western countries are both centralized and capital-intensive: nuclear, synfuel, oil shale, and expanded coal-burning. None of these offers any particular benefit to women and most promise actual harm. Expanded burning of coal and synthetic fuels will increase air pollution and enhance the 'greenhouse effect,' in which the production of carbon dioxide contributes a layer of insulation that raises the temperature of the earth (Large, 1980). Harvesting solar energy through solar cells in space sounds promising, until the potential health and environmental hazards of microwaving energy to earth are considered. The nuclear power industry has not yet shown the capability to safely dispose of radioactive wastes.

These consequences are of particular concern to women: women are slated to remain the primary caretakers of the young and the old, the disabled and the infirm. Whether as unpaid wives, mothers, and daughters, or as paid nurses, physical therapists, teachers and counsellors, women are responsible for providing the special nurturing and assistance needed by victims of genetic or environmental hazards. Since a woman's reproductive system includes a life-time supply of eggs, even one-time exposure to radiation or chemical pollution can permanently harm the genetic structure of all future offspring. [Men continually produce new supplies of sperm (Warnock, 1979b).] Rather than making, the workplace safe for everyone, companies are now using this susceptibility to discriminate against women (*New U.S. Guidelines on Reproductive Hazards*, 1980).

The determination of a national energy policy demands a close analysis of which population groups are 'at risk' physically or financially. Women have not been able to move into the forums in which energy policy is being determined. There are small groups of women working with appropriate technologies (e.g. Feminist Resources on Energy and Ecology in Syracuse, New York, Women in Solar Energy in Vermont, the North Fork Confluence of Feminists and Environmentalists in Montana), and many other women working within alternative organizations which remain male-dominated (e.g. Ecotope Group in Seattle, RAIN in Oregon, the National Center for Appropriate Technology in Montana).[8]

But when government has sought feminist assistance in energy policy, it has focused on women's role as an energy consumer, not as policy-maker. For example, the U.S. government, together with Consumer Action Now (CAN), a New York-based information group, tried to set up a program of energy conservation targeted at women's economic needs (Cimons, 1979). According to Maura O'Neill, assistant director of CAN:

'We need to sell conservation and renewable resources. To do that, we have to target a specific audience. We have chosen women ... Women play an instrumental role in managing family budgets and could be very effective in reducing energy use in the residential sector.'

Thus, in energy, the area of technology which receives the noisiest press, the voices of women are conspicuously, and perhaps lethally, silent.

PAPA, MAMA, AND BABY MAKES TWO

Today's news is filled with stories of contraceptive disasters: blood clots from birth control pills, infections from IUD's, abuse of sterilization procedures. Tomorrow's news will be filled

---

[8] A more extensive listing can be found in Judy Smith's booklet *Something Old, Something New, Something Borrowed, Something Due*, 1978.

instead with stories about the technology of conception, which will have as great an impact on female futures in the 21st century as the control of pregnancy has had in this one.

Artificial insemination. Sperm banks. *Ex utero* fertilization (test tube babies). Surrogate mothers. Genetic screening. Amniocentesis. *In vitro* fetal development (artificial wombs). The words rocket out from science fiction fantasy to the borders of reality, and they are rocketing at speeds faster than the ethical light it takes to comprehend them.

Reproductive technology seems to provide additional options for women who want children but cannot, or choose not to, conceive through intercourse. Surrogate pregnancy allows women who cannot, or do not want to, maintain a preganancy to have a biological child. Genetic screening of parents and amniocentesis, the analysis of fluid surrounding a fetus, provide information on the chances of healthy fetal development vs the development of genetic malformation or hereditary disease which would create heartache and suffering for the child in its lifetime. Feminist theorists and writers have postulated such technologies as prerequisites for female freedom. Shulamith Firestone in *The Dialectic of Sex* (1970) suggested mechanical wombs; Joanna Russ in *The Female Man* considered ova fusion and parthenogenesis as alternative modes of reproduction (1975).

While such technologies may offer women freedom from childbearing, which has been a form of female bondage, they also offer men an unprecedented opportunity to assert control over the one aspect of the life process which has eluded them until now. In all other aspects of health-care, mechanization and technology has resulted, intentionally or inadvertently, in the destruction of female dominance over traditional female spheres of activity: male pharmacists supplanted female herbalists; male obstetricians, female midwives (Rich, 1976). Men have a long record of usurping control of medical technologies (Ehrenreich and English, 1979).

A combination of effective genetic screening, cloning, and *in vitro* fertilization could remove women from the reproductive process altogether. By cloning only males, screening for those with blue eyes, blond hair and Aryan build, the horror of a eugenically determined population becomes more than the demented mania of a tyrant, but a fearful and awesome possibility.

Genetic technology recently received a boost from a 1980 decision of the U.S. Supreme Court (*Diamond vs Chakrabarty*, 1980). Based on the Court's decision to permit the patenting of new life forms, private biological laboratories, operating outside Federal regulations, see a period of exponential economic growth ahead (Bishop, 1980; Mann, 1980; Whitefield, 1980). In a capitalistic economy, the potential for making money provides its own impetus for the development and production of new inventions, including living things, regardless of the use to which those inventions may later be put. The gene-splicing (recombinant DNA) technique that creates oil-spill-eating bacteria or interferon to fight cancer, and the implantation technique that permits the introduction of new insulin-producing cells into a diabetic patient are also techniques which provide essential information needed to implant a full complement of chromosomes, carrying only desired genes, in an egg or sperm cell.

The prospect is far more perturbing than anything Jacques Ellul might have had in mind when he called ours 'a civilization commited to the quest for continually improved means to carelessly examined ends' (Ellul, 1964, p. vi). Whether or not one agrees with Firestone's or Russ' vision of a future without biological motherhood, one must examine carefully the probability that reproductive technologies will be developed without women's active involvement, informed consent, or even awareness.

For all their potential value, reproductive technologies, like those of computers, telecommunications, and energy, offer women glitter without goal achievement. Unless women gain control of the development of these technologies, they will find they have created new lives for themselves today, only to have forfeited the future—an empty womb indeed.

A TIME FOR ACTION, A TIME FOR HOPE

Like Gramsci, the founder of the Italian Communist Party, I believe that 'one must make a pessimistic analysis of the situation, but when it's time for action, one must act with hope.' Given the inertial momentum of the technological process, I do not believe that it will be possible for women to stop the development of any of the technologies described here. Nor do I believe that trying to stop technology is the answer. It is all too easy for the industrialized Western nations, which predicate their future profits on advanced technology, scornfully to write off women 'outsiders' as Luddites (in the early nineteenth century Luddites tried to prevent industrialization in England by destroying machinery).

But women can park themselves in the path of technological determinism. They can call the lie claiming that the laws of nature decree how technology must be applied. They can name the processes of male-defined politics that determine what projects will be funded, what research items will be subsidized by the government, what priorities will be set, whose needs will be served.

To subvert some of these technologies to their own ends, women must extend their spheres of organization and influence beyond the traditional social service concerns of the women's ghetto. They must educate themselves in science and mathematics and start to chip off projects which use and control technologies to their own ends.

Women must remain alert to efforts to co-opt feminist concepts to support male-implemented technologies, even those which are considered ecologically or environmentally sound, unless they have a voice in determining the development and application of the proposed alternatives. Some theorists, like Nancy Jack Todd, link soft, appropriate technologies with women's biological experience (Todd, 1980) or with traditional female values of cooperation, small-scale development, and life-enrichment. Such theorists ignore the fact that a similar case can be made for the feminine nature of high technology electronic systems, which can be receptive, inter-active, non-linear, simultaneous, and multi-channel; electronic systems are linearly and hierarchically designed by those (men) with the power to structure them.

As women press for involvement at the highest levels of technological policy planning, they must recognize and resist attempts to fragment the women's movement from the outside. The Mormons tried it in Houston; it was attempted in Copenhagen. Manipulatively denying consideration of women's common concerns in favor of male-structured policies and priorities, plays into patterns of male domination and oppression.

Technological development, hence product expansion, is a cornerstone of capitalism. To subvert developmental goals to meet women's needs may be the only path to survival in this economic system. Playing games with high technology means playing with guns, not butter. It is the game of the multi-nationals, from Mobil to Mitsubishi and Rockwell to RCA. The alternatives are no less than terrifying. Women will find themselves dealing with the world of tomorrow using yesterday's tools, the technological hand-me-downs of their brothers; they will find themselves racing toward the technological horizon, only to see it receding before them. To refuse to acknowledge the dominance of technology in economic structures and daily life—to return home to build a solar oven, to grow a garden and bake bread, to retreat to self-sufficiency and labor-intensive survival in a beautiful, but small and unrealistic world—is to leave those who already hold the chips playing the game; it is to leave the weapons of female destruction in the hands of men whom history has shown willing to pull the trigger.

REFERENCES

Allen, Donna. 1980. First satellite teleconference by women. *Media Report to Women* **8**, 1–2.
Banking From Home. 1980. *IEEE Spectrum* **17**, 78.
Behind AT & T's Change at the Top. 1978. *Business Week* November 6, pp. 115–126.
Bishop, Jerry. 1980. Gene-splicing field is swiftly approaching the commercial stage. *The Wall Street Journal* June 24.
Bose, Christine. 1979. Technology and changes in the division of labour in the American home. *Women's Studies Int. Q.* **2**, 295–384.
Caswell, Stephen. 1978. Satellites and the automated office. *Satellite Communications* **2** (1), 40–47.
Cimons, Marlene. 1979. Teaching women about energy. *Los Angeles Times* March 28.
Daly, Mary. 1978. *Gyn/ecology: the Metaethics of Radical Feminism*. Beacon Press, Boston.
Densmore, Dana. 1978. Can a computer by your sister? *MS* **7** (11), 102–118.
Densmore, Dana. 1979. Women called to enter computer field. *Media Report to Women* **7** (7), 4.
Ehrenreich, Barbara and English, Deirdre. 1979. *For Her Own Good*. Anchor Press/Doubleday, Garden City, New York.
Ellul, Jacques. 1964. *The Technological Society*. Alfred A. Knopf, New York.
Firestone, Shulamith. 1970. *The Dialectic of Sex*. Bantam, New York.
Galbraith, John Kenneth. 1973. *Economics and the Public Purpose*. Houghton Mifflin, Boston.
Greene, Bob. 1980. How much is a hosewife worth? *Los Angeles Times* September 19.
Griffin, Susan. 1978. *Woman and Nature: the Roaring Inside Her*. Harper and Row, New York.
Hill, Arthur. 1978. CATV and satellites: the sky is the limit. *Satellite Communications* **2** (12), 20–25.
Howe, Louise Kapp. 1977. *Pink Collar Workers*. Avon Books, New York.
Kazickas, Jurate and Sherr, Lynn. 1980. *The Woman's Calendar for* 1980. Universe Books, New York.
Large, Arlen. 1980. Weather report: more heat. *The Wall Street Journal* August 1.
Learn More From Your T.V. Read It. 1980. Advertisement by Prestel Int. *Scientific American* **243** (2), 20.
Lockheed Corporation. 1980. *Database Catalog*. Dialog Information Retrieval Service. Palo Alto, Calif.
MacFadyen, J. Tevere. 1980. The future: a Walt Disney production *Next* **1** (3), 24–32.
Mann, Jim. 1980. Scientists may patent life made in lab. *Los Angeles Times* June 17.
Margulies, Lee. 1977. Cable TV experiment launched. *Los Angeles Times* December 21.
Margulies, Lee. 1979. All-news TV coming into view. *Los Angeles Times* May 23.
McCormack, Margaret. 1977. A feminist perspective. *Social Policy* December 18.
Merchant, Carolyn. 1980. *The Death of Nature*. Harper and Row, San Francisco.
Morgan, Robin. 1980. Sisters at a summit. *Los Angeles Times* August 3.
New U.S. Guidelines on Reproductive Hazards. 1980. *Women's Occupational Health Resource Center News* 2, 1 and 4.
Project Opens Computer Science Jobs to Women. 1980. *Computer World* July 28, pp. 16–17.
Reece, Ray. 1980. The solar blackout. *Mother Jones* **5** (8), 28–37.
Rich, Adrienne. 1976. *Of Woman Born: Motherhood as Experience and Institution*. W. W. Norton, New York.
Rosenthal, Peter. 1980. Personal computers in the home. Address at Wescon/80 Convention, September 16.
Russ, Joanna. 1975. *The Female Man*. Bantam, New York.
Samuelson, Robert J. 1980. Are the managers mismanaging? *Los Angeles Times*. August 5.
Schultz, Brad. 1980. Programmers seen needing fewer skills. *Computer World* July 28, pp. 1–6.
Schumacher, E. F. 1973. *Small Is Beautiful*. Harper and Row, New York.
Shaffer, Richard. 1980. Home, office wiring to carry lots more than current(ly). *The Wall Street Journal* July 25.
Smith, Judy. 1978. *Something Old, Something New, Something Borrowed, Something Due*. National Center for Appropriate Technology, Butte, MT.
Smythe, Dallas. 1976. Communications: blind spot of western Marxism. Circulated paper, Simon Fraser University.
System Development Corporation. 1978. *Orbit Databases*. SDC Search Service. Santa Monica, Calif.
Todd, Nancy Jack. 1980. Tomorrow is our permanent address. Circulated address, New Alchemy Institute.
Toffler, Alvin. 1980. *The Third Wave*. William Morrow, New York.
TV with a Phone. 1980. *IEEE Spectrum* **17**, 78.
U.S. Dept. of Commerce. 1977. NTI Search. National Technical Information Service, Springfield, Virginia.
U.S. Supreme Court. 1980. *Diamond vs Chakrabarty*. 79–136.

Warnock, Donna. 1979a. *What Growthmania Does to Women and the Environment*. Feminist Resources on Energy & Ecology, Syracuse, New York.

Warnock, Donna. 1979b. *Even Nukes Discriminate Against Women*. Feminist Resources on Energy & Ecology. Syracuse, New York.

Whitefield, Debra. 1980. Patent decision could spur genetic research industry. *Los Angeles Times* June 17.

Xerox Corporation. 1979. *Xerox Xten*. Promotional Brochure. Tarzana, Calif.

Zimmerman, Jan. 1977. Women and satellites. National Women's Agenda. New York.

Zimmerman, Jan. 1978. Women and satellites. *Media Report to Women* **6** (7), 4–10.

Women's Studies Int. Quart., Vol. 4, No. 3, p. 369, 1981.
Printed in Great Britain.

0148–0685/81/030369–01$02.00/0
Pergamon Press Ltd.

WOMEN'S STUDIES

TEACHING AND LEARNING ABOUT WOMEN AND TECHNOLOGY

JOAN ROTHSCHILD

University of Lowell, Lowell, Massachusetts, U.S.A.

A recent arrival on the Women's Studies scene, women and technology as a field for teaching and learning, has now definitely taken hold. Courses are included in academic departments, as well as in Women's Studies curricula and in growing numbers of multi-disciplinary science and technology programs. There are a few special women/technology programs, and feminist networks have developed. A key feature of educational work in this area is the way in which the subject matter lends itself to going beyond the traditional classroom setting, as means and methods are developed to empower women firsthand with technological knowledge and skills. Programs have been initiated to encourage female interest in and train women for jobs in technical fields once virtually closed to women.

Facilitating such educational activity are special women's organizations, often formed within existing professional societies, that help to focus the new research and teaching through establishing networks, conferences and programs, and organizing panels at professional meetings. Notable among these organizations are the Association of Women in Science, established a decade ago, and Women in Technological History (WITH), formed in 1976 by Martha Moore Trescott and members of the Society for the History of Technology (SHOT). (Mailing address for the WITH newsletter is: Gay Bindocci, College of Mineral and Energy Resources, West Virginia University, Morgantown, WVA 26506.) Caucuses and/or women's committees also exist within a number of the professional science associations, such as the History of Science Society, Philosophy of Science Association, and the American Physical Society. The Society of Women Engineers, established in 1952, and the Society of Women Geographers, going back to 1925, rank among the lonely foremothers of these newer women's science and technology organizations. In San Diego, California, a feminist Computer Network is underway to set up data storage and retrieval systems on women's resources and to initiate training workshops. Spring 1981 brought two West Coast conferences: 'Technology and the Future of Women' at the Women's Studies Program of San Diego State University, and 'The Way of the Future—Planning and Technology' sponsored by the Northwest Region Women's Studies Association at Oregon State University.

The following represent several approaches to teaching and learning about women and technology.

Women's Studies Int. Quart., Vol. 4, No. 3, pp. 370–372, 1981.
Printed in Great Britain.

0148–0685/81/030370–03$02.00/0
Pergamon Press Ltd.

FEMINIST PEDAGOGY AND TECHNOLOGY: REFLECTIONS ON THE GODDARD FEMINISM AND ECOLOGY SUMMER PROGRAM

YNESTRA KING[1]

Goddard College,[2] Plainfield, VT 05667, U.S.A.

During the summer of 1980 I coordinated the first program to combine feminism and ecology in a women's studies program. The program announcement said:

'This summer a new program begins at Goddard College, the Feminism and Ecology summer program. It reflects the convergence of the two major political movements of the '70s, feminism and environmentalism, and their challenge to the technological imperative which underlies the death-oriented aspects of our society.

The goal of the program is to develop a life-centered, healing movement for the '80s. We will concern ourselves with feminist theory, art, technology, politics and health. Students will work with prominent visiting faculty and take courses in appropriate technologies (solar, wind energy, efficient shelter), holistic health and nutrition, biological agriculture and aquaculture, feminist theory and women's history.

Recent political developments threaten to accelerate the arms race, bring back the draft, further the development of nuclear power and spur the backlash against feminist and ecological activism. Those of us concerned with life must speak out and develop the ideas, tools, and vision we will need to act publicly as women always have privately, for life on earth. Join us.'

Although the program was not advertised until late April, 25 students arrived on 3 June to begin the 12 week residency. By all accounts the program was an outstanding success. In the final evaluation session student after student said that the program had changed their lives. Many of them are continuing to work together on projects generated out of the summer, including organizing for a Women's Pentagon Action (against militarism, held 16–17 November 1980), entering apprenticeships in solar energy, energy retrofitting, and holistic health programs, and pursuing theoretical work in feminist philosophy and anthropology.

The program emphasized personal transformation—the empowering of our women students in all aspects of their lives as a first step toward social transformation. We attempted to engage every aspect of the person, and, given the often overwhelming pace and diversity of the program, we succeeded. The program demanded total involvement, and students and

---

[1] Ynestra King is a social theorist and a long time feminist and ecological activist. She is currently at work on a book on feminism and ecology, and teaches at Goddard College, in Plainfield, VT, U.S.A. She co-founded Women and Life on Earth, a northeast coalition for feminism and ecology. Last year she coordinated the Conference on Women and Life on Earth which brought together women activists, theorists, workers and artists to explore how women are affected by and affect ecological concerns, and to found the coalition. Write to Women and Life on Earth, 160 Main Street, Northampton, MA 01060, U.S.A. for further information.

[2] Goddard College is a private co-ed, progressive liberal arts college in northern New England with a commitment to the arts and social change.

faculty alike were occupied from early in the morning until late in the evening. Program issues and themes were discussed continuously, women helped each other with projects and papers, and there was a rollicking social life in the dorm. We pushed the students hard and created a context of seriousness. I think they benefitted from this concentrated context much more than women students who sandwich feminist courses into conventional curricula and attempt to piece together the various expressions of their feminist perspective on their own. The age span of the students was great—the class and race diversity less so, although more than half of our students received some financial aid.

Students attended classes daily, which involved them in 'hands on' projects in appropriate technology and biological agriculture and aquaculture, there were guest speakers every afternoon, and in the evenings they attended classes which addressed the philosophical and political issues involved in developing an ecological feminist theory and practice. The program emphasized the critical and reconstructive dimensions of feminist social change. The 'critical' included social criticism and political activism, and the reconstructive included developing vision, tools and technologies needed to create a society based on feminist and ecological principles. Throughout the program there were visiting feminist artists who worked collaboratively in the landscape with students and brought an aesthetic perspective to our reconstructive vision.

Visiting faculty, all of whom stayed with students in the women's dorm for a few days and were available on an informal basis as well as during their lectures, included prominent feminists from a number of academic disciplines, social movements, and ecologically oriented professions. Randy Forsberg, Director of the Institute for Defense and Disarmament Studies, spoke on the weapons race and feminism and disarmament. Susan Griffin (1978), author of *Woman and Nature*, talked about the process of researching and writing her book and gave a workshop on women and writing. Anna Gyorgy (1979), prominent anti-nuclear activist and author of *No Nukes: Everyone's Guide to Nuclear Power*, gave organizing workshops and discussed the international anti-nuclear movement. Grace Paley, long time peace activist and feminist writer, read from her work, and talked about links between her work as a peace activist and her feminist philosophy. Peggy Taylor, editor of *New Age* magazine, which concerns itself with holistic health, talked to students about opportunities in the field and gave workshops on various self-healing techniques. Nancy Jack Todd, co-founder of the New Alchemy Institute,[3] delivered a moving talk on 'A Conspiracy for Gaiia' and the work of the New Alchemists in developing what she called a 'healing science for Gaiia'. (Gaiia is a metaphor for the planet Earth and all its interconnected inhabitants.) Pat Hynes, environmental engineer, inspired students with slides of a greenhouse she had designed and built herself, and spoke on feminism and ecology. Rosemary Ruether, prominent humanist theologian, delivered a series of talks on feminist ecological ethics and visions for the future.

The Feminism and Ecology Summer Program is connected with the Institute for Social Ecology at Goddard College and makes use of Goddard's appropriate technology teaching facility (Cate Farm) with its gardenes, numerous greenhouses, aquaculture systems, and building facilities for 'hands on' work. At certain times of the day various facilities or workshops were designated 'women only', and students were given special instruction and support designed to help them overcome the insecurities common to women who take up tools, and begin to learn about technology for the first time. Students in the tools and

---

[3] The New Alchemy Institute is a research and teaching facility on Cape Cod, Massachusetts, based on ecological principles and engaged in energy efficient, decentralized food production.

construction class for women built sets and props for the end-of-summer Women's Cultural Celebration, an all day exhibition of women's art work, and class projects.

There were no 'women only' classes in the technology area of the program; these were held in cooperation with the Social Ecology Program. I think this was a mistake. Women often had a hard time in classrooms with men who were more confident than they, even with a feminist instructor. Next summer there will be 'women only' courses in the technical areas. There was also a bit of strain between students in the Social Ecology Summer Program and students in the feminist program over why there needed to be an autonomous feminist program, why there were occasional closed sessions with faculty and women students, and overt sexist language in the classroom. The 'program within a program' status of the feminist program meant that feminist faculty were often doing double duty—running interference and educating the campus at large, and attempting to meet the special needs of women students.

Everything in our experience last summer confirms that programs like the Feminism and Ecology Summer Program are needed. However, our experience also suggests that the more autonomous they can be the better. It's very difficult for women to learn about technologies, or to develop a feminist epistemology and critique of technology in a mixed context. The men are more confident and verbal than the women, and more fluent in the discourse of technological issues. As we continue with the program we would like to develop a feminist pedagogy for teaching women the technologies so that they can begin to enter the male-dominated trades which pervade the appropriate technology field. We would also like to combine a feminist ecological aesthetic with practical designs, and to develop an ecological feminist critique of technology. The program is a conceptual and pedagogical breakthrough for feminist studies and ecological programs because we have identified the promise and the problems of combining these in an educational endeavor. Of course, there are the same problems and many more in attempting to bring together the feminist and ecological political movements, but this program is instructive even there. Feminist studies programs must broaden their concerns, and teach women practical skills in classrooms illuminated by feminist politics and pedagogy. Although teaching women the skills they need to participate in social reconstruction (technical, social, political, etc.) is a logical direction for feminist studies, the Goddard program is unique in attempting to extend academically oriented women's studies in this direction. It also shows the importance of feminist social criticism to ecology, and the interest of feminists in being part of the ecology movement broadly conceived.

For further information on the Feminism and Ecology Summer Program write: Admissions, Goddard College, Plainfield, VT 05667, U.S.A. There is a slide tape documentation of last summer's program available to interested groups.[4]

REFERENCES

Griffin, Susan. 1978. *Woman and Nature: The Roaring Inside Her.* Harper & Row, New York.
Gyorgy, Anna. 1979. *No Nukes: Everyone's Guide to Nuclear Power.* South End Press, Boston.

---

[4] Although inquiries and projected enrolments in the feminist program showed that the program would be extremely successful, Goddard College's over-riding, long-term financial difficulties led to a decision in May of 1981 by the Goddard Board of Trustees to not offer any summer programs in 1981. Therefore the Feminism and Ecology Summer Program was not offered in 1981 as Goddard's decision came too late for us to find another affiliation for summer 1981.

We are currently seeking another institutional affiliation and expect to continue elsewhere in the summer of 1982.

Women's Studies Int. Quart., Vol. 4, No. 3, pp. 373–374, 1981.
Printed in Great Britain.

0148–0685/81/030373–02$02.00/0
Pergamon Press Ltd.

A PREVIEW OF AAUW's BIENNIAL STUDY/ACTION TOPIC 'TAKING HOLD OF TECHNOLOGY'

CORLANN GEE BUSH

University of Idaho, Moscow, Idaho 83843, U.S.A.

Not all teaching in Women's Studies is conducted in an academic setting. Women's clubs and organizations have long provided a forum for continuing education for women. While the actual, local meetings of women's clubs frequently feature demonstrations of flower arrangement techniques or slides of a member's trip overseas, the national leadership of some women's organizations consciously attempts to involve their members in woman-centered learning. One such group is the American Association of University Women, an organization of over 190,000 members from approx. 2000 branches.

Every 2 years the Association undertakes study/action programs on topics of current interest to its members. For the past decade, these topics have been extremely timely and relevant. For example, recent topics have dealt with 'World Pluralism', 'The Politics of Food', and 'Managing Resources for Tomorrow'. Beginning in July 1981, the topics will concern economics, 'Money Talks', and technology, 'Taking Hold of Technology'. These topics were selected as a result of an Association-wide interest assessment process that is conducted every 2 years by the Program Development Committee of the Association.

It is significant that an organization such as AAUW selected technology as a topic for in-depth study. First, it indicates that women are becoming intested in a subject that has heretofore been the exclusive domain of white, male professionals. Second, it demonstrates that women want to understand and have a voice in the technological innovations and decisions that affect their lives. Finally, it bespeaks their frustration with existing analyses and assessments of technology that have neglected and ignored women's special needs and concerns.

The goals for the 2-year study action topic are summarized below:

EDUCATION:
(1) To overcome technology anxiety through participation in hands-on, experiential activities.
(2) To analyze the connections and contradictions between feminism and technology.
ASSESSMENT:
(1) To acquire skills to assess the benefits and risks of technology.
(2) To begin a feminist assessment of technology.
ACTION:
(1) To identify and explore opportunities to implement technology in private lives and in community activities.
(2) To educate others—particularly young women—about technology and assist others in overcoming technology anxiety.
(3) To influence technological decision-making by serving on boards, commissions, task forces, etc.

In order to accomplish these goals, the topic materials presented to members will focus on the following subjects:

(1) history and philosophy of
    technological development;
(2) feminism and technology;
(3) appropriate technology;

(4) bio/medical technology;
(5) energy technology;
(6) information/communications technology;
(7) computer literacy.

Connections will be drawn among these content areas and the Association's on-going commitments to cultural interests, community development, education and international relations.

All this is not to imply, however, that there will be no resistance to the technology topic or to its obviously feminist perspective. Technology anxiety runs deep, and some members will doubtless prefer to avoid the subject entirely or feel it is not a 'woman's issue'. Conversely, many Association members will see in this topic an appealing, safe, male-approved escape from a decade of political activism in support of women's rights. Still others will welcome the topic as long as it deals with gadgets (computers, video recorders, electronic games, etc.) but will reject it when the values, assumptions and decisions of the technocratic establishment are questioned. Thus, steering a middle course that will help women overcome their technology anxiety and, at the same time, develop a feminist critique of technology presents a difficult but welcome challenge.

For additional information, please contact: American Association of University Women, 2401 Virginia Avenue NW, Washington, DC 20037, U.S.A., or Corlann Gee Bush, Chair, 'Taking Hold of Technology' Topic Committee. 414 South Lincoln Street, Moscow, ID 83843, U.S.A.

Women's Studies Int. Quart., Vol. 4, No. 3, 374–377, 1981.
Printed in Great Britain

0148–0685/81/030374–04$02.00/0
Pergamon Press Ltd.

TEACHING WOMEN AND TECHNOLOGY AT THE UNIVERSITY OF WASHINGTON

CHRISTINE BOSE

State University of New York (SUNY) at Albany, New York

PHILIP BEREANO and IVY DURSLAG

University of Washington, Seattle, WA

'Women and Technology' began as a course in the Social Management of Technology Program and the Sociology Department at the University of Washington in spring 1976 and was repeated in the springs of 1977, 1978 and 1980. It is now cross-listed with Women's

Studies as well. It will be taught regularly every other year as an interdisciplinary upper-wider graduate and graduate level course. Thus, although enrolment varies from 7 to 20, the course has achieved a regular place in the curriculum. Female/male ratios range from two-thirds to three-quarters female. 'Women and Technology' does not directly influence departmental courses, but its impact is large on students whose curriculum might otherwise be quite standard. Science and engineering students learn to see the values embedded in their work, while women studies students learn not to reject technology out of hand and rather to understand the many ways technologies can work for or against women. Over the last few years this course has developed teaching and substantive components which help to do this and to make it a model course.

'Women and Technology' has always been taught by an interdisciplinary female/male team. The faculty have come from backgrounds in social management of technology, sociology and political science, with all having had some participation in Women's Studies. This interdisciplinarity provides an essential synthesis since social and technical sciences have defined and viewed technology differently historically. Of course, this team approach helps draw students from a diversity of majors, and they can teach and learn from each other. This component is structured into the course such that part of a student's grade is based on presenting one of the later class sessions, using the assigned reading as a base to integrate material and raise important questions for discussion. Other course requirements include class participation and writing a research paper.

The substantive aspects of the course cover many diverse areas and much reading is required beyond the three texts (Garson, 1972, *All the Livelong Day*; Dickson, 1975, *The Politics of Alternative Technology*; Ehrenreich and English, 1979, *For her Own Good*). The course begins by setting up an analytic framework which will help to understand the case studies used later. Although the students are initially resistant to this theoretical component, its essential nature is clear by the end of the course. Theory is presented in three ways. First, mainstream and radical approaches to the definition of technology and its relationship to society are examined through authors as diverse as Peterson (1973), Bell (1973), Mesthene (1970), Kuhn (1970), Dickson (1975), Bookchin (1971) and Braverman (1974). Next, women's relationship to technology and change is briefly examined in pre-industrial, industrializing and industrial societies. This segment allows us to survey how technologies have or have not controlled, or been controlled by, women for their own needs. The final portion of this opening section looks at technology and values. Two disparate sets of values are compared. Scientific rationality is viewed as reductionism or breaking down into parts (exemplified in the factory system) which comes from a need to dominate and is based on an estrangement from nature. Works by Frankel (1973), Henderson (1975) and Roszak (1974) help to illustrate and criticize this set of values for its inability to solve social problems. On the other hand, a feminist holistic and integrating approach [represented by Firestone (1970), and Dolkart and Hartstock (1975)] is contrasted as one which considers that subjective factors and a totalistic approach to problem-solving are important.

The next section of 'Women and Technology' comprises a large part of the course. Entitled 'The Division of Labor', it looks at the impacts of technology on the home and workforce labor of women. The section opens with a discussion of the family and the relationship of its members to paid and unpaid work. The development of paid work and the molding of the nineteenth-century workforce itself is examined. Next, the effects of technology and industrialization on women are seen through the eyes of authors such as Gilman (1966), Davies (1974), Guilbert (1970) and Braverman (1974). To illustrate the personal effects of industrialization, vignettes of contemporary women's work by Garson (1972), Terkel (1974), Langer (1970) and others are then discussed. Another theory interlude follows here by using works of authors such as Baxandall *et al.* (1976), Hartmann (1976), Blau and Jusenius (1976), and Boulding (1976). These help explain the mass of data on industrialization's impact on women in the workforce and the home. This discussion both ties together the previous weeks' readings on women in the workforce and prepares for a discussion of technology and housework.

Many aspects of housework are explored, beginning with its social and technological history. Current working conditions, which include the time involved, technology used and ideology, are then summarized using selections from the burgeoning numbers of recent works such as those by Oakley (1975), Vanek (1974), Walker and Woods (1976), Burns (1976), Cowan (1974, 1976a, 1976b) and Berk *et al.* (1976). A following section examines consumerism as a contemporary major component of housework; and finally, the strategy of wages for housework is discussed as one approach (which is clearly better than the 'technology for housework' strategies) to improving the homemaker's status.

The last section of the course focuses on biomedical technologies which particularly affect women: birthing, birth control, abortion, and the male medical establishment's ability to define sickness and health. Readings by Ehrenreich and English (1973a, 1973b), Arditti (1974), Gordon (1977a, 1977b) and Rich (1976) are used for this purpose.

By this point the course has fully integrated a mass of theoretical and substantive reading from several disciplines. A feminist and anti-reductionist view towards technology has also been developed and supported. Students have both read much and done some original research and synthesis of materials. After several years of teaching this course, we feel it is very successful.

Nonetheless, there are a few problems or issues of which other users of this course framework should be aware. First, students are resistant to the volume of diverse reading which this interdisciplinary approach requires. Aiming the course at more advanced students helps mitigate this problem, while giving introductions to the disciplinary approach of some of the authors is also recommended. Second, students tend to be issue-oriented and do not initially like the theoretical components. This is in part due to the fact that many of our students are in the 'hard' sciences and have no previous training in critical or social science analysis. It takes them several weeks to understand that biology, engineering, physics and the like are not entirely 'objective', but in fact are perspectives, approaches or paradigms themselves. On the other hand, some feminist students resist any mode of analysis as a form of male thinking. It takes time for both types of students to be able to see the several ways of approaching the relationship of women and technology, and patience is advised here. Finally, if there were more time available for the course, we would expand it to include new areas. In particular, we would recommend examining how women's issues relate to other technology-related movements in general, such as the anti-nuclear one. We would look at technologies not traditionally associated with women.

If you would like further information on 'Women and Technology', write to: Philip Bereano, Social Management of Technology FS-15, University of Washington, Seattle, Washington 98195.

REFERENCES

Arditti, Rita. 1974. Women as objects—science and sexual politics. *Science for the People*. 8–11 September, pp. 29–32.

Baxandall, Rosalyn, Ewen, Elizabeth and Gordon, Linda. 1976. The working class has two sexes. *Monthly Review* **28**, July–August, pp. 1–9.

Bell, Daniel. 1973. Five dimensions of post-industrial society. *Social Policy*. July–August, pp. 103–110.

Berk, Sarah F., Berk, Richard A. and Berheide, Catherine W. 1976. The non-division of household labor. Northwestern University, Evanston, IL. Unpublished.

Blau, Francine D. and Jusenius, Carol. 1976. Economists' approaches to sex segregation in the labor market: an appraisal. In: Blaxall, Martha and Reagan, Barbara eds, *Women and the Workplace*. pp. 181–199. University of Chicago Press, Chicago.

Bookchin, Murray. 1971. *Post-Scarcity Anarchism*. Ramparts Press, San Francisco.

Boulding, Elise. 1976. Familial constraints in women's work roles. In: Blaxall, Martha and Reagan, Barbara eds. *Women and the Workplace*. pp. 95–117. University of Chicago Press, Chicago.

Braverman, Harry. 1974. *Labor and Monopoly Capital: The Degradation of Work in the Twentieth Century*. Monthly Review Press, New York.

Burns, Scott. 1976. The shift from a market economy to a household economy. *Co-Evolution Quarterly*. Fall, pp. 18–29.

Cowan, Ruth Schwartz. 1974. A case study of technological and social change: the washing machine and the working wife. In: Hartman, Mary S. and Banner Lois eds. *Clio's Consciousness Raised*. pp. 245–253. Harper & Row, New York.

Cowan, Ruth Schwartz. 1976a. The 'industrial revolution' in the home: household technology and social change in the 20th century. *Technology and Culture* **17**, January, pp. 1–23.

Cowan, Ruth Schwartz. 1976b. Two washes in the morning and a bridge party at night: the American housewife between the wars. *Women's Studies* **3**, 147–172.

Davies, Margery. 1974. Woman's place is at the typewriter: the feminization of the clerical workforce. *Radical America* **8** (4), July–August.

Dickson, David. 1975. *The Politics of Alternative Technology*. Universe Books, New York.

Dolkhart, Jane and Hartsock, Nancy. 1975. Feminist visions of the future. *Quest: a feminist quarterly* **II** (1), Summer, pp. 2–6.

Ehrenreich, Barbara and English, Deirdre. 1973a. *Complaints and Disorders: The Sexual Politics of Sickness*. Feminist Press, Old Westbury, New York.

Ehrenreich, Barbara and English, Deirdre. 1973b. *Witches, Midwives, and Nurses: A History of Women Healers*. Feminist Press, Old Westbury, New York.

Ehrenreich, Barbara and English, Deirdre. 1979. *For Her Own Good: 150 Years of the Experts' Advice to Women*. Anchor Press/Doubleday, Garden City, New York.

Firestone, Shulamith. 1970. *The Dialectic of Sex: The Case for a Feminist Revolution*. William Morrow, New York.

Frankel, C. 1973. The nature and sources of irrationalism. *Science*. NY, 1 June, pp. 927–931.

Garson, Barbara. 1972. *All the Livelong Day*. Penguin Books, Baltimore, MD.

Gilman. Charlotte Perkins. 1966. *Women and Economics*. Harper & Row, New York.

Gordon, Linda. 1977a. Birth control: an historical study. *Science for the People*, Jan–Feb, pp. 11–16.

Gordon, Linda. 1977b. Birth control and the Eugenists. *Science for the People*, March–April, pp. 8–15.

Guilbert, M. 1970. Women and work (III): the effects of technological change. *Impact of Science on Society*, April/June, pp. 85–91.

Hartmann, Heidi. 1976. Capitalism, patriarchy, and job segregation by sex. In: Blaxall, Martha and Reagan, Barbara eds. *Women and the Workplace*, pp. 137–169. University of Chicago Press, Chicago.

Henderson, Hazel. 1975. Philosophical conflict: re-examining the goals of knowledge. *Public Administration Review*, Jan–Feb, pp. 77–80.

Kuhn, Thomas S. 1970. *The Structure of Scientific Revolutions*. 2nd edn, enl. University of Chicago Press, Chicago.

Langer, Elinor. 1970. *The Women of the Telephone Company*. New England Free Press, Somerville, MA.

Mesthene, Emmanuel. 1970. *Technological Change*. New American Library, New York.

Oakley, Ann. 1975. *Woman's Work: The Housewife, Past and Present*. Pantheon Books, New York.

Peterson, Richard A. 1973. *The Industrial Order and Social Policy*. Prentice-Hall, Englewood Cliffs, New Jersey.

Rich, Adrienne. 1976. *Of Woman Born: Motherhood as an Experience and Institution*. W. W. Norton, New York.

Roszak, Theodore. 1974. The monster and the Titan: Science, knowledge, and gnosis. *Daedalus*, Summer, pp. 17–32.

Terkel, Studs. 1974. *Working*. Pantheon, New York.

Vanek, Joann. 1974. Time spent in housework. *Scientific American* **231** (5), 116–120.

Walker, Kathryn E. and Woods, Margaret E. 1976. *Time Use: A Measure of Production of Family Goods and Services*. Center for the Family of the American Home Economics Association, Washington, DC.

Women's Studies Int. Quart., Vol. 4, No. 3, pp. 378–379, 1981.
Printed in Great Britain.

0148–0685/81/030378–02$02.00/0
Pergamon Press Ltd.

WOMEN AND TECHNOLOGY PROJECT, MISSOULA, MONTANA

The Women and Technology Project, working out of the Women's Resource Center in Missoula, Montana, under the leadership of Judy Smith, includes in its work the development of conferences, courses, publications, and networks. Courses are prepared for presentation at other locations, such as a summer course on Women and Appropriate Technology at Southern Oregon State College in 1980; lectures on appropriate technology and technology assessment from a feminist perspective are offered nationwide.

At the Women and Technology conference held at the University of Montana in April 1979, Elizabeth Coppinger (1979, p. 24) described appropriate technology in this way:

'Appropriate technology deals with issues of local control ... to allow people and communities to have the power to decide what is appropriate for them. Appropriate technology promotes energy conservation and the use of renewable resources; local food production ... local economic control ... [I]n order to be truly appropriate, something must be appropriate for everyone, not just for white males. If it's not appropriate for women, it's not appropriate. If it's not appropriate for poor people, for minorities, its not appropriate, it's simply passing the oppression on from one group to another.'

The following is the statement of the Clark Fork Confluence of Feminists and Environmentalists, a network emerging from the Women and Technology Project:

'The Clark Fork Confluence of Feminists and Environmentalists is a network of women living in the Northwest who are involved in making connections between feminism and environmentalism, women's roles and technology. We have organized several roundtables for feminists and environmentalists in Montana in which participants have attempted to identify the commonalities and differences between the feminist movement and the ecology movement and set up two ways to facilitate cooperation between the two. In spring, 1979, we organized a conference "Women and Technology: Deciding What's Appropriate" [at the University of Montana] and a Women and Technology Network. We have produced two publications, *Something Old, Something New, Something Borrowed, Something Due: Women and Appropriate Technology* [Smith, 1980] and *Conference Proceedings: Women and Technology: Deciding What's Appropriate* [1979] and have made a number of presentations at feminist and environmentalist meetings. We are currently designing a Women and Appropriate Technology Workshop which we hope to offer in a variety of communities in Montana.

We are interested in presenting our discussion to as wide an audience of feminists and environmentalists as possible. Although the feminist movement and the ecology movement both state they are working to create a future society where people have more personal control over their life choices, we have found there has been minimal communication between the movements. Few groups in either movement have analyzed the other movement's concerns or made steps to build coalitions and share resources. Recently some feminists have been working with the anti-nuclear movement, but there has not been a reciprocal move by ecologists to work on feminist projects. We feel the timing is crucial, that the chance for coalition or synergy exists, but that a great deal of education must be done so that feminist priorities are not sacrificed.

Questions we are addressing include: What has been the impact on women's roles of modern, energy-intensive technology? How has it expanded women's roles? How has it limited women's roles? We need a sex role impact statement as well as an environmental impact statement for technological and energy developments. What would be the impact on women's roles of a return to less energy-intensive technology? What would women be required to give up? What factors have kept women from participating in scientific and technological decision-making (e.g. science and math anxiety, limited access to training and skills)? How can women insure that their interests are represented in this decision-making process? Does the ecology/alternative technology movement address the needs and concerns of women? Why are the theorists, leaders and decision-makers in these movements mostly men? How can women make sure these movements address the concerns of women? Can the feminist movement and the ecology movement work together? Are their priorities really that close together? How can feminists work with other movements without sacrificing their own priorities?

'We are very interested in contacting others who share our concern in building connections between the feminist and ecology movements, recognizing that the priorities and resources of both must be integrated if there is to be a chance to achieve a non-sexist, ecologically-sane future. For further information, write to us at 315 S. 4th E., Missoula, Montana 59801.'

REFERENCES

Conference Proceedings: Women and Technology: Deciding What's Appropriate. 1979. Women's Resource Center, Missoula, Montana.

Coppinger, Elizabeth. 1979. Women and appropriate technology. In: *Conference Proceedings: Women and Technology: Deciding What's Appropriate*, p. 24.

Smith, Judy. 1980. *Something Old, Something New, Something Borrowed, Something Due: Women and Appropriate Technology*. Women and Technology Network, Missoula, Montana. (Originally published 1978. National Center for Appropriate Technology, Butte, Montana).

INDEX